Thermokarst and Thaw-Related Landscape Dynamics—An Annotated Bibliography with an Emphasis on Potential Effects on Habitat and Wildlife

By Benjamin M. Jones, Courtney L. Amundson, and Joshua C. Koch, U.S. Geological Survey; and Guido Grosse, University of Alaska–Fairbanks

Compiled for the Arctic Landscape Conservation Cooperative

Open-File Report 2013–1161

U.S. Department of the Interior
U.S. Geological Survey

U.S. Department of the Interior
SALLY JEWELL, Secretary

U.S. Geological Survey
Suzette M. Kimball, Acting Director

U.S. Geological Survey, Reston, Virginia: 2013

For more information on the USGS—the Federal source for science about the Earth,
its natural and living resources, natural hazards, and the environment—visit
http://www.usgs.gov or call 1–888–ASK–USGS

For an overview of USGS information products, including maps, imagery, and publications,
visit *http://www.usgs.gov/pubprod*

To order this and other USGS information products, visit *http://store.usgs.gov*

Suggested citation:
Jones, B.M., Amundson,C.L., Koch, J.C., and Grosse, Guido, 2013, Thermokarst and thaw-related
landscape dynamics—An annotated bibliography with an emphasis on potential effects on habitat and
wildlife: U.S. Geological Survey Open-File Report 2013-1161, 60 p., http://pubs.usgs.gov/of/2013/1161.

Contents

English-Language Literature 3

Russian-Language Literature 58

Acknowledgments 59

Conversion Factors

Inch/Pound to SI

Multiply	By	To obtain
Length		
foot (ft)	0.3048	meter (m)
Flow rate		
inch per year (in/yr)	25.4	millimeter per year (mm/yr)

SI to Inch/Pound

Multiply	By	To obtain
Length		
centimeter (cm)	0.3937	inch (in.)
millimeter (mm)	0.03937	inch (in.)
meter (m)	3.281	foot (ft)
kilometer (km)	0.6214	mile (mi)
Area		
square meter (m^2)	0.0002471	acre
hectare (ha)	2.471	acre
square meter (m^2)	10.76	square foot (ft^2)
hectare (ha)	0.003861	square mile (mi^2)
square kilometer (km^2)	0.3861	square mile (mi^2)
Volume		
cubic meter (m^3)	264.2	gallon (gal)
cubic meter (m^3)	1.308	cubic yard (yd^3)
cubic kilometer (km^3)	0.2399	cubic mile (mi^3)
cubic meter (m^3)	0.0008107	acre-foot (acre-ft)
cubic hectometer (hm^3)	810.7	acre-foot (acre-ft)
Flow rate		
centimeter per day (cm/d)	0.3937	inch per day (in/d)
centimeter per year (cm/yr)	0.3937	inch per year (in/yr)
meter per day (m/d)	3.281	foot per day (ft/d)
meter per year (m/yr)	3.281	foot per year ft/yr)
millimeter per year (mm/yr)	0.03937	inch per year (in/yr)
Biomass		
metric ton per hectare (t/ha)	0.446	ton per acre (ton/acre)

Temperature in degrees Celsius (°C) may be converted to degrees Fahrenheit (°F) as follows:

°F=(1.8×°C)+32.

Thermokarst and Thaw-Related Landscape Dynamics— An Annotated Bibliography with an Emphasis on Potential Effects on Habitat and Wildlife

By Benjamin M. Jones, Courtney L. Amundson, and Joshua C. Koch, U.S. Geological Survey; and Guido Grosse, University of Alaska–Fairbanks

Permafrost has warmed throughout much of the Northern Hemisphere since the 1980s, with colder permafrost sites warming more rapidly (Romanovsky and others, 2010; Smith and others, 2010). Warming of the near-surface permafrost may lead to widespread terrain instability in ice-rich permafrost in the Arctic and the Subarctic, and may result in thermokarst development and other thaw-related landscape features (Jorgenson and others, 2006; Gooseff and others, 2009). Thermokarst and other thaw-related landscape features result from varying modes and scales of permafrost thaw, subsidence, and removal of material. An increase in active-layer depth, water accumulation on the soil surface, permafrost degradation and associated retreat of the permafrost table, and changes to lake shores and coastal bluffs act and interact to create thermokarst and other thaw-related landscape features (Shur and Osterkamp, 2007). There is increasing interest in the spatial and temporal dynamics of thermokarst and other thaw-related features from diverse disciplines including landscape ecology, hydrology, engineering, and biogeochemistry. Therefore, there is a need to synthesize and disseminate knowledge on the current state of near-surface permafrost terrain.

The term "thermokarst" originated in the Russian literature, and its scientific use has varied substantially over time (Shur and Osterkamp, 2007). The modern definition of thermokarst refers to the process by which characteristic landforms result from the thawing of ice-rich permafrost or the melting of massive ice (van Everdingen, 1998), or, more specifically, the thawing of ice-rich permafrost and (or) or melting of massive ice that result in consolidation and deformation of the soil surface and formation of specific forms of relief (Shur, 1988). Jorgenson (2013) identifies 23 distinct thermokarst and other thaw-related features in the Arctic, Subarctic, and Antarctic based primarily on differences in terrain condition, ground-ice volume, and heat and mass transfer processes. Typical Arctic thermokarst landforms include thermokarst lakes, collapsed pingos, sinkholes, and pits. Thermokarst is differentiated from thermal erosion, which refers to the erosion of the land surface by thermal and mechanical processes (Mackay, 1970; van Everdingen, 1998). Typical thermal erosional features include thermo-erosional gullies. Thermal abrasion is further differentiated from thermokarst and thermal erosion by association with the reworking of ocean, river, and lake bluffs (Are, 1988). Typical thermo-abrasion features include erosional niches at the base of bluffs. Thermal denudation is another distinct term that refers to the effect of incoming solar energy on the thaw of frozen slopes and permafrost bodies that subsequently become transported downhill by gravity (Shur and Osterkamp, 2007). Active layer detachment slides and thaw slumps are typical thermal denudation features. Shur and Osterkamp (2007) noted that these various transport processes may occur together with thermokarst or in instances that would not be considered thermokarst.

This compilation of references regarding thermokarst and other thaw-related features is focused on the Arctic and the Subarctic. References were drawn from North America as well as Siberia. English-language literature mostly was targeted, with 167 references annotated in version 1.0; however, an additional 28 Russian-language references were taken from Shur and Osterkamp (2007) and are provided at the end of this document. This compilation may be missing key references and inevitably will become outdated soon after publication. We hope that this document, version 1.0, will serve as the foundation for a comprehensive compilation of thermokarst and permafrost-terrain stability references, and that it will be updated continually over the coming years.

English-Language Literature

1. **Agafonov, L., Strunk, H., and Nuber, T., 2004, Thermokarst dynamics in western Siberia: Insights from dendrochronological research: Palaeogeography, Palaeoclimatology, Palaeoecology, v. 209, p. 183–196.**
   This paper describes the use of dendrochronological techniques for reconstructing the formation of one thermokarst depression in the boreal forest region of western Siberia. Wood samples were collected from the Siberian stone pine from three different settings: a steep frozen slope that showed several leaning trees, a thermokarst depression where most trees had been killed owing to submergence, and a control site on the plain above the slope. A total of approximately 40 trees were sampled among the three sites. Based on the timing of tree mortality from the center of the depression outwards, the thermokarst was determined to have been formed in the early 1900s and had expanded laterally at rates ranging from 4 to 8 cm/yr with the highest rates occurring during the 1920s and 1930s and associated with some of warmest air temperatures of the 20th century. However, during the second half of the 20th century, rates of 7 cm/yr have been inferred, a result of increased precipitation rather than increase air temperature.

2. **Allard, M., 1996, Geomorphological changes and permafrost dynamics—Key factors in changing arctic ecosystems—An example from Bylot Island, Nunavut, Canada: Geoscience Canada, v. 23, no. 4, p. 205-212.**
   This paper summarizes several soil and geomorphological factors formed since the Holocene that may affect Arctic ecosystems and possibly could be used to inform a permafrost monitoring program. Bylot Island, Nunavut, Canada, is used as an example site. Peat-rich soils can assist in interpreting past changes related to the intensity of geomorphological processes. Accumulation of peat and sand is closely related to aggradation of permafrost and frost cracking, leading to tundra polygons. Buried vegetation layers beneath drained lake sediments show changes to lake inundation and drainage, and pingo formation. Eolian activity may increase in colder and drier periods. Based on soil core samples obtained from many sites on Bylot Island, areas of the island support a dynamic and sensitive assemblage of polygons, thaw lakes, and pingos that have changed continuously over the last 3,000 years. Surface changes including geomorphology and vegetation in a network of sensitive sites, along with climate and permafrost temperature monitoring, constitute a comprehensive method to assess the affect of climatic changes on land systems. However, precision mapping of polygon and vegetation types, and measurements of peat thickness and composition are vital components for adequately monitoring permafrost feature changes.

3. **Are, F.E., 1988, Thermal abrasion of sea coasts: Polar geography and geology, v. 12, no. 1, p. 1-81, no. 2, p. 87-157.**
   These papers present information on the thermal abrasion of ice-rich permafrost coasts in Siberia. The author focuses on the shape and height of the coastal bluffs, coastal retreat rates, and subsequent lowering of the sea bed. He finds that erosion rates along these ice-rich coastal bluffs are 3–4 times higher than along comparable non-frozen sediments. The long-term mean retreat rate for ice-rich coastal bluffs is 10 m/yr and maximum observed rates are about 50 m/yr in some extreme cases.

4. **Arp, C.D., Jones, B.M., Schmutz, J.A., Urban, F.E., and Jorgenson, M.T., 2010, Two mechanisms of aquatic and terrestrial habitat change along an Alaskan Arctic coastline: Polar biology, v. 33, no. 12, p. 1629-1640.**

This paper examines how coastal erosion and storm-surge flooding are affecting coastal Arctic ecosystems in the Teshekpuk Lake Special Area, Alaska (N-TLSA). Long-term observational records and recent short-term monitoring data were analyzed to quantify erosion rates, coastal lake drainage, and amount of salt-burned tundra in the N-TLSA. They used remote sensing, Systeme Pour l'Observation de la Terre (SPOT) data, and aerial photographs to examine erosion rates and habitat changes. Nearby weather data were used to examine the history of storm events. Pressure transducers were placed at lakes and near-shore ocean locations to record water levels and water temperature in 2007. Water-quality surveys and soil-temperature thermistors also were used intermittently at a subset of lakes from 1977 to 2009 to monitor water levels and temperatures. The erosion rate of the coastline has accelerated, ranging from 6 m/yr during 1955–1979 to 17 m/yr during 2007–2009. Intensive monitoring indicates high interannual variability in erosion and flooding events. The frequency and magnitude of storm events is increasing and corresponds to more lake tapping (draining) and flooding events since 2000. The paper estimates that 6 percent of the landscape consists of salt-burned tundra, while 41 percent is vulnerable to storm-surge flooding. Westerly storms create extensive flooding, while easterly storms have negligible effects on lakes and coastal tundra. Flooding and storm surges are converting coastal freshwater lakes into brackish lakes and estuaries, which affects vegetation and aquatic communities near the coast.

5. **Arp, C.D., Jones, B.M., Urban, F.E., and Grosse, G., 2011, Hydrogeomorphic processes of thermokarst lakes with grounded ice and floating ice regimes on the Arctic coastal plain, Alaska: Hydrological Processes, v. 25, no. 15, p. 2422–2438.**

This paper uses field surveys, remote sensing, and hydrological modeling to assess the relative role of lake expansion and water balance on the surface area change of 13 thermokarst lakes north of Teshekpuk, on the Arctic Coastal Plain of northern Alaska over a 35-year period. The 13 lakes were distinguished based on depth and whether the lake experienced grounded-ice or floating-ice conditions during the winter period. Shoreline expansion rates were determined by comparing late-1970s aerial photography with a 2002 orthophoto dataset. Expansion rates ranged from a mean of less than 0.2 m/yr in shallow lakes to 1.8 m/yr in the deeper lakes, while the mean annual expansion rate for all lakes was 0.9 m/yr. Mean lake depth and mean shoreline erosion rate were correlated (coefficient of determination [R^2] is 0.73, p-value is less than 0.01) in this region. The erosion of the 13 lake basins resulted in an increase in surface area of 3.2 percent. A multi-temporal time series of Landsat Thematic Mapper and Enhanced Thematic Mapper Plus images at 30-meter resolution also were assessed for these 13 lakes in an attempt to link changes in surface area to specific conductance measures and modeling of water balance. However, this analysis was limited because of the relatively coarse resolution associated with the Landsat imagery and the inability to accurately resolve feature edges. It was generally determined that the expansion of these lakes owing to permafrost degradation masked the changes in water balance, with the exception of two shallow lakes with a stable basin. Based on the modeling results of water balance, divergent longer-term patterns of water balance were indicated in shallow lakes compared to deep lakes in the region.

6. **Arp, C.D., Whitman, M.S., Jones, B.M., Kemnitz, R., Grosse, G., and Urban, F.E., 2012, Drainage network structure and hydrologic behavior of three lake-rich watersheds on the Arctic Coastal Plain, Alaska: Arctic, Antarctic, and Alpine Research, v. 44, no. 4, p. 385–398.**
    This paper highlights the importance of lakes and drained-lake basins on the hydrological response in watersheds located on the low-lying Arctic Coastal Plain of northern Alaska. The study area consisted of three primary watersheds, Fish Creek, Judy Creek, and the Ublutuoch River, with a total drainage basin area of about 4,600 km^2. Most streams in these watersheds initiate from lake basins, about one-third of the lakes are connected to the fluvial drainage network, and between 17 and 26 percent of the watershed drainage density is in lake basins. Rainfall runoff and drought responses also were affected by the proportion of the landscape covered by lakes relative to drained thaw lake basins (DTLBs). Comparison of snowmelt and base flow recession from a broader set of Alaskan North Slope watersheds showed little relationship to drainage area, but significant variation was accounted for by static lake area extent. This high and varied level of stream-lake connectivity likely plays a role in the distribution of aquatic ecosystems and fish communities across this landscape.

7. **Balser, A.W., Gooseff, M.N., Jones, J.B., and Bowden, W.B., 2009, Thermokarst distribution and relationships to landscape characteristics in the Feniak Lake region, Noatak National Preserve, Alaska: Final Report to the National Park Service, Arctic Network, Fairbanks, Alaska, December 31, 2009, p. 1-12.**
    This gray literature report details the distribution of thermokarst features for a 3,600-square-kilometer area centered on Feniak Lake in the Noatak National Park and Preserve in the Brooks Range of Alaska. This region represents a transitional landscape between arctic and alpine tundra, and boreal shrubland. The methods used in this study were low-altitude helicopter surveys, ground surveys, low-altitude vertical aerial photography, and analysis of historical Alaska high-altitude photography (AHAP) program images. Mapping of thermokarst features in the field involved measures of length, width, depth at headwall, aspect, and slope, and description of vegetation in and around thermokarst features. Mapping of thermokarst features in the recent and historical aerial photographs was done manually following georectification of the photography to a Landsat 7 Enhanced Thematic Mapper Plus image of the study region. The accuracy of the rectification and the horizontal location of mapped thermokarst features were about 4 meters. Based on the aerial photo mission from 2006, the authors mapped 503 thermokarst features in the Feniak Lake study area that included active layer detachment slides (389), retrogressive thaw slumps (79), thermokarst gullies (28), and glacial thermokarst features (7). When comparing the features from 2006 to the features apparent aerial photography from about the 1980s period, the authors observed a twofold increase in the number of thermokarst' features over the 25-year period. The distribution of the thermokarst features aligned well with various landscape associations based on slope, land cover, and lithology. In particular, thermokarst features were observed almost exclusively on non-carbonate lithologies and in wet sedge meadow and low shrub-tussock tundra. The increase in thermokarst features was attributed to more frequent periods of hot, sunny summer weather. The authors also noted the presence of several stabilized thermokarst features that likely represented past periods of permafrost thaw in the region.

8. **Benninghoff, W.S., 1952, Interaction of vegetation and soil frost phenomena: Arctic, v. 5, no. 1, p. 34–44.**

   This paper describes the influence of frozen soils on the establishment and propagation of vegetation communities, and the converse of this. Frozen soils exert great force and trauma on root systems of plants through repeated freeze-thaw cycles, differential frost heaving, cracks caused by rapid freezing, and so on. Plants have adapted shallow root systems to adapt to impervious permafrost, which make trees and shrubs easy to overturn in inclement weather or wind storms. Insufficient depth for the proper functioning of roots limits spruce forest, and species with flexibility of their root habits are most likely to establish themselves in permafrost areas. Furthermore, plants may be subjected to severe water loss by exposure to drying winds while roots are encased in frozen soil and cannot absorb water, which may also be a contributing factor that limits tree growth in permafrost terrain. Thermokarst features caused by the melting of variable amounts of ice in the soil change the physical environment for vegetation occupying a site. Margins of lakes with high permafrost tables are particularly susceptible to destruction, In the Nebesna, Chisana, and Tanana River valleys of eastern Alaska, previous research estimated mean shore retreat of 2.3–7.5 in./yr. The oriented lakes of the Arctic Coastal Plain were shown as constantly changing, owing to caving of shores, draining, filling with peat, and initiation of new thaw cycles. All permafrost areas are characterized by the instability of the surface and consequent transience of site conditions. Vegetation also influences frozen soils. It shields the soil from maximum penetration of heat through shading, decreases air circulation, retains moisture in and just above the soil, prevents thaw through root systems, intercepts rain, and cools the soil through evaporation of moisture on plant surfaces. Mosses may play an important part in this effect. Removal of moss, thick turf, and surface peat greatly hastens thawing of frozen ground. However, vegetation also can warm soils by impeding heat radiation from the soil to the cold air and retaining snow cover, which insulates the ground from lower temperatures. Vegetation may be important for reducing frost disturbance in tundra through anchoring roots to the soil and the insulating effects of the aboveground plant parts. Because of soil frost changes following disturbance, the affected surface and the local environment may change so much that entirely different communities occupy the site for unknown time periods.

9. **Billings, W.D., and Peterson, K.M., 1980, Vegetational change and ice-wedge polygons through the thaw-lake cycle in arctic Alaska: Arctic and Alpine Research, p. 413–432.**

   This paper provides an overview of the thermokarst lake cycle through the study of vegetation succession in a chronosequence of drained thermokarst lake basins near Barrow, Alaska. Pioneer species in recently drained lake basins consisted of *Dupontia fischerii* and *Arctophila fulva*. As time passes since drainage, *Carex aquatilis* becomes more abundant as does the development of ice-wedge polygonal networks.

10. **Bilodeau, F., Reid, D.G., Gauthier, G., Krebs, C.J., Berteaux, D., and Kenney, A.J., 2012, Demographic response of tundra small mammals to a snow fencing experiment: Oikos, doi:10.1111/j.1600-0706.2012.00220.x.**

Models predict snow cover will increase in the Arctic with warmer temperatures. Brown and collared lemmings, which prefer deep snow for winter nesting and to avoid predation, may benefit from additional snow depth. However, foxes could focus on areas with greater small mammal abundance and counteract any gains for small mammals from deeper snow cover. This study experimentally manipulated snow cover using snow fences to examine potential effects of deeper snow cover on small mammal populations in the Canadian Arctic. Small mammal nest density was 1.5 times greater in experimental areas, but gains did not mean larger populations, more lactating females or signs of reproduction in winter nests, or greater numbers of juveniles in the spring. The authors speculate that once snow melted, lemmings redistributed themselves to take advantage of summer forage. Results on predation were inconclusive.

11. **Black, R.F., 1969, Geology, especially geomorphology, of northern Alaska: Arctic, v. 22, p. 3, p. 283–299.**

This paper provides a broad overview of the geomorphology of northern Alaska from the Brooks Range to the Arctic Coastal Plain, with an emphasis on the role of the Naval Arctic Research Laboratory in the region. Because much of this early work was concentrated around Barrow, Alaska, the two most important landforms studied were the oriented lakes and ice-wedge polygons. Many hypotheses about the oriented lakes near Barrow were reviewed. The author helped resolve a debate on the formation of ice wedges with the help of his wife Herelda. The paper offers many suggestions for future geomorphological studies in the region.

12. **Black, R.F., 1969, Thaw depressions and thaw lakes, a review: Biuletyn Peryglacjalny, v. 19, p. 131–150.**

This review paper provides an overview on the state of knowledge regarding thermokarst depressions and thermokarst lakes in the late 1960s. Much effort was spent studying thermokarst lakes in the late-1950s and throughout the 1960s, based primarily in Barrow, Alaska. Instead of citing all this literature, we have chosen to cite this review paper because it references all this literature. This paper provides details on the background of thermokarst lake-related research, a synopsis of the processes responsible for their formation and drainage, and suggestions for future study.

13. **Bowden, W.B., 2010, Climate change in the Arctic–Permafrost, thermokarst, and Why They Matter to the Non-Arctic World: Geography Compass, v. 4, no. 10, 1553-1566, doi: 10.1111/j.1749-8198.2010.00390.x.**

This paper presents an overview on the arctic environment, permafrost characteristics, and the role of thermokarst features as indicators of current climate change and as possible agents of future change. The paper presents information on a few thermokarst landforms however there is no information on rates of change or spatial distribution. The paper concludes with a section on thermokarst in a changing Arctic from a systems perspective. A diagram of the role of thermokarst in the evolution of an Arctic landscape in a warmer and wetter climate is shown in figure 5 of the paper. This paper is geared to the non-Arctic community.

14. **Bowden, W.B., Gooseff, M.N., Balser, A., Green, A., Peterson, B.J., and Bradford, J., 2008, Sediment and nutrient delivery from thermokarst features in the foothills of the North Slope, Alaska—Potential impacts on headwater stream ecosystems: Journal of Geophysical Research, v. 113, G02026, doi: 10.1029/2007JG000470.**

Thermokarst features are increasing near the Toolik Lake Natural Research Area, and these features are delivering nutrients and sediments to headwater streams. These additions are at levels that are well above background levels, and at concentrations that have been found to significantly affect primary and secondary production in water bodies. Although thermokarst features only affect a finite area on the terrestrial landscape, their effects may be felt throughout a very large fraction of the stream network. Thermokarsting increased small-stream total suspended sediments (TSS) by several orders of magnitude, and increased Toolik River TSS by about one order of magnitude. Nutrients increased downstream of thermokarst features, and remained elevated for several hundred meters downstream. Sampling of another nearby feature indicated that nutrient outflows from thermokarst features have elevated stream concentrations of nutrients during the period of record (1999–2005).

15. **Burn, C.R., 1992, Thermokarst lakes: Canadian Geographer-Le Géographe Canadien, v. 36, no. 1, p. 81–85.**

This paper provides an overview of thermokarst lakes as a primary example of thermokarst landforms in regions that contain ice-rich permafrost. Information is provided on lake initiation and development, the thermal regime of lakes and its effects on permafrost temperature, and the cessation of lake growth and ultimately lake drainage. Lake expansion rates of about 0.7 m/yr were noted from a previous study focused on lakes near Mayo, Canada. The author noted the extensive Russian literature on the subject, much of which has not been translated, and the usefulness of monitoring and studying thermokarst lakes as they are a surface expression of the response of permafrost to climate change.

16. **Burn, C.R., 2000, The thermal regime of a retrogressive thaw slump near Mayo, Yukon Territory: Canadian Journal of Earth Sciences, v. 37, no. 7, p. 967–981.**

This paper presents details on the formation and stabilization of a retrogressive thaw slump in Canada through the use of detailed field studies and instrumentation. Date loggers were installed in the slump floor and in undisturbed terrain. The temperature of the slump floor was warmer in both the summer and winter, and the net result was 4°C warming of the ground. The dominant mode of heat transfer in the thaw slump was conduction. Information also was presented on permafrost aggradation in a stabilized thaw slump in the region.

17. **Burn, C.R., 2002, Tundra lakes and permafrost, Richards Island, western Arctic coast, Canada: Canadian Journal of Earth Sciences, p. 39, no. 8, p. 1281–1298.**
This paper describes the role of tundra lakes on permafrost conditions for a location on Richards Island in the western Canadian Arctic. The author reports water and lake-bottom temperature measurements, the configuration of permafrost, and active layer thicknesses from 1992 to 1997 for one site. The lake study site consists of a deep central pool with shallow littoral shelves. The annual mean temperature measured at the lake bottom in the central pool ranged from 1.5°C to 4.8°C, depending on depth, and from -0.2°C to -5°C on the terraces, owing to differences in snow cover and nearness to the central pool. Therefore, the temperature of permafrost at a depth of 7 m in the terraces also varied, from -2°C near shore to -5°C in mid-terrace. The active layer in the terraces was uniformly 1.4 m deep. Geothermal modeling based on the field data indicates that there likely is a through-going talik below the central pool. Scaling this observation to the rest of the island, at least 10–15 percent of the island was underlain by a talik.

18. **Burn, C.R., 2005, Lake-bottom thermal regimes, western Arctic coast, Canada: Permafrost and Periglacial Processes, v. 16, no. 4, p. 355–367.**
This paper presents lake-bottom temperature data for two lakes with littoral shelves, a residual pond in a drained lake basin, and a lake located in the taiga. Temperature data were collected over several years. Lake-bottom annual mean temperatures were greatest for the taiga lake (5°C) owing to the lack of ice growth in the winter. The tundra lakes with littoral shelves had mean annual temperatures of about 3°C in the deep central part of the lake and -2°C in the littoral shelves. Given projected warming in the region, the tundra lakes may transition to resemble the thermal regime of taiga lakes, and this will affect talik configuration.

19. **Burn, C.R., and Friele, P.A., 1989, Geomorphology, vegetation succession, soil characteristics and permafrost in retrogressive thaw slumps near Mayo, Yukon Territory: Arctic, p. 31–40.**
This paper describes two active and one stable retrogressive thaw slumps formed along a river-cut bank that flows through ice-rich, glaciolacustrine sediments in the Yukon Territory. Field surveys were combined with aerial photography to document the development of the two active thaw slumps since 1949, vegetation succession on the floors of all three slumps, and the short-term soil development on surfaces of various ages in the slumps. All slumps were thought to have been formed after riverbank erosion exposed the ice-rich sediment. Since the start of the two active thaw slumps, mean headwall retreat has varied between 12 and 14 m/yr, with maximum retreat rates of 16 m/yr. Measured retreat rates of thaw slump headwalls for various locations in the Arctic range from 1 to 18 m/yr (table 2 in this paper). The reestablishment of plant communities is associated with the initiation of soil development in fresh soil substrata and is well advanced after 40 years succession of closed-spruce forest.

20. **Burn, C.R., and Smith, M.W., 2006, Development of thermokarst lakes during the Holocene at sites near Mayo, Yukon Territory: Permafrost and Periglacial Processes, v. 1, no. 2, p. 161–175.**

This paper describes the formation of thermokarst lakes in the boreal forest region of the Yukon Territory using ground surveys, remote sensing, and dendrochronology. The paper describes the growth of thermokarst lakes through analysis of aerial photography and tree-ring series obtained from submerged trees in the expanding lake margins. The mean axial growth rate of 16 thermokarst lakes is presented in table 1. The mean growth of lakes was 0.7 m/yr along their long axis and 0.5 m/yr along their short axis. The maximum observed expansion rate was 1.2 m/yr. The expansion rate of lakes likely is not constant from year to year and, during particularly warm summers, stable banks may be reactivated and lake expansion may accelerate. Tree-ring analysis and measurements of lake talik thickness indicate that the lakes likely formed in the mid-1800s. Estimates of talik formation indicated vertical degradation of permafrost of about 0.5 to 1 m/yr. The authors provided a context in which to interpret the formation of thermokarst lakes in the region throughout the Holocene and suggested that these lakes likely were formed following a forest fire.

21. **Cabot, E.C., 1947, The northern Alaskan coastal plain interpreted from aerial photographs: Geographical Review, v. 37, no. 4, p. 639–648.**

This paper describes the utility of black and white, vertical and oblique aerial photography for describing permafrost-related landforms in northern Alaska. There is a brief discussion on the formation of lakes and ponds in the region, elongation of lakes, drainage of lakes, and a lake cycle. The author noted the role of floating lake ice pans and mechanical erosion of shorelines in the expansion of lakes and the role of bank overflow during breakup as a key process for lake drainage.

22. **Chen, W., Chen, W., Li, J., Zhang, Y., Fraser, R., Olthof, I., .and Chen, Z., 2012, Mapping Aboveground and Foliage Biomass Over the Porcupine Caribou Habitat in Northern Yukon and Alaska Using Landsat and JERS-1/SAR Data, Remote Sensing of Biomass - Principles and Applications, Dr. Lola Fatoyinbo (Ed.), ISBN: 978-953-51-0313-4, InTech, DOI: 10.5772/19219.**

This article used Landsat imagery and remote sensing techniques to map the aboveground biomass and foliage biomass of the range of the Porcupine caribou herd. The area includes part of the Arctic Wildlife Refuge on the Arctic Coastal Plain, Alaska, and western Yukon and Northwest Territories, Canada. Field studies were done to ground-truth satellite images in the middle of the growing season. Habitat characteristics were measured and those characteristics were related to satellite images of the same area to predict biomass across the entire range. Measured aboveground biomass ranged from 10 to 100 t/ha for sparsely forested woodlands, 1 to 100 t/ha for low-high shrub sites, and 0.5 to 10 t/ha for mixed graminoids-dwarf shrub-herb sites. Biomass was similar on the calving and breeding grounds for the Porcupine caribou herd, which was greater than what is available to the Bathurst caribou herd. This may explain partially why the Bathurst herd leaves their calving grounds soon after giving birth, while the Porcupine herd stays at their calving grounds much longer, and Porcupine herd calves grow faster and weigh more than Bathurst herd calves.

23. **Chen, M., Rowland, J.C., Wilson, C.J., Altmann, G.L., and Brumby, S.P., 2012, Temporal and spatial pattern of thermokarst lake area changes at Yukon Flats, Alaska: Hydrological Processes, online publication, 10.1002/hyp.9642.**
This paper provides further evidence that lakes in the Yukon Flats region of Alaska have dynamic surface areas. Closed-basin lakes were selected from Landsat data acquired between 1984 and 2009 for a 422-km^2 study area. Eighty percent of the variation in surface water area was explained by local water balance and mean temperature following snowmelt. Nearly 14 percent of the change during the study period was determined to represent long-term change. The authors hypothesized that most of the lake change resulted from the presence or absence of ice-jam flooding.

24. **Christensen, T. R., Johansson, T., Åkerman, H. J., Mastepanov, M., Malmer, N., Friborg, T., Crill, P., and Svensson, B. H., 2004, Thawing sub-arctic permafrost— Effects on vegetation and methane emissions, Geophysical Research Letters, v. 31, no. 4, L04501.**
This paper examines changes in methane fluxes from 1970 to 2000 associated with increasing active-layer depths and a change in vegetation type and distribution. Vegetation shifted from shrub-dominated, elevated, ombrotrophic conditions to wet, graminoid-dominated, nutrient-rich, minerotrophic conditions, corresponding to changes in the underlying permafrost distribution. Historical methane fluxes were estimated given field-measured methane fluxes determined from individual vegetation types using chamber fluxes. The microtopographical and hydrological changes indicated by vegetation change have increased the landscape scale methane emissions by 22–66 percent over this 30-year period. Regional differences may be important, as permafrost thaw may lead to drying and, therefore, decreased methane emissions in some locations.

25. **Costard, F., Gautier, E., Brunstein, D., Hammadi, J., Fedorov, A., Yang, D., and Dupeyrat, L., 2007, Impact of the global warming on the fluvial thermal erosion over the Lena River in Central Siberia: Geophysical Research Letters, v. 34, no. 14, L14501.**
This paper links climatic changes in Central Siberia to fluvial erosion of the Lena River. Three major changes since the 1980s are noted: reduced winter ice thickness, increased spring water temperature (up to 2°C), and a slight increase in spring discharge. Areal and satellite maps were used to observe the effects of these fluvial changes on the riverbanks and vegetated islands. The most obvious change was accelerated head retreat in vegetated islands, which increased by 21–24.5 percent. These rates are consistent with predictions from an ablation model, from which it was determined that the water temperature increase was a 4-times-more important explanatory variable than the discharge increase. Deposition of sediments on wide bars and long islands suggests that eroded sediment is not transported far, but means that islands migrate faster.

26. **Czudek, T., and Demek, J., 1970, Thermokarst in Siberia and its influence on the development of lowland relief: Quaternary Research, v. 1, no. 1), p. 103–120.**
This paper presents an overview on the development of thermokarst landforms and their role in lowering the elevation of the regional land surface in the Siberian lowlands. Two modes of thermokarst development are distinguished: (1) back-wearing and (2) down-wearing. Back-wearing refers to the lateral development of thermokarst features and results in the formation of gullies, thermocirques, and slump head walls. Down-wearing refers to formation of thermokarst through an increase in the active-layer thickness or the top-down thaw of permafrost that leads to development of "alas" terrain. Back-wearing features tend to be more local in nature and down-wearing features tend to be more regional in nature. The extent of the geomorphic changes for all thermokarst features depends on the tectonic regime of the region (stable, rising, or lowering), the ice content of the soil and the presence of epigenetic or syngenetic permafrost, and the rate of disequilbrium disturbance or the disturbance to the ground thermal regime. The paper has several diagrams showing the formation of various thermokarst features. This paper is mostly descriptive in nature and does not contain information on the rates of thermokarst formation nor the regional distribution.

27. **Daanen, R.P., Grosse, G., Darrow, M.M., Hamilton, T.D., and Jones, B.M., 2012, Rapid movement of frozen debris-lobes—Implications for permafrost degradation and slope instability in the south-central Brooks Range, Alaska. Natural Hazards and Earth System Sciences, v. 12, p. 1521–1537.**
This paper describes reconnaissance-level investigations of unusual debris mass movement features (referred to as "frozen debris-lobes") in the south-central Brooks Range of Alaska. A combination of ground-surveys, remote sensing, and field and laboratory measurements, and time-lapse observations were used to document the movement indicators that include toppling trees, slumps and scarps, detachment slides, striation marks on frozen sediment slabs, buried trees and other vegetation, mudflows, and large cracks in the lobe surface. Some of the frozen debris lobe features are greater than 100 m in width, 20 m in height, and 1,000 m in length. The features have responded to climate change by increasing in their downslope movement during the last several decades. Mean annual rates of movement were from 2 to 4 m/yr over decadal time periods. The features showed signs of creep, slumping, viscous flow, blockfall and leaching of fines in warm seasons; and creep and sliding of frozen sediment slabs in cold seasons. The potential hazard of one frozen debris lobe feature as it encroached on the Dalton Highway was highlighted.

28. **Dallimore, S.R., Wolfe, S.A., and Solomon, S.M., 1996, Influence of ground ice and permafrost on coastal evolution, Richards Island, Beaufort Sea coast, NWT: Canadian Journal of Earth Sciences, v. 33, no. 5, p. 664–675.**
This paper provides information on the role of ground ice on coastal change for Richards Island, Canada. Excess ice content for the coastal segment was estimated at 20 percent and, when this was considered, the balance between headland erosion and coastal deposition was in near equilibrium. The coastal part eroded by thermo-mechanical niche erosion and block collapse as well as permafrost slumping. Parts of the coast with higher ice content tended to erode faster than less ice-rich coastal area. Mean annual coastal erosion rates ranged from 1 to 2 m/yr between 1947 and 1985.

29. **Dupeyrat, L., Costard, F., Randriamazaoro, R., Gailhardis, E., Gautier, E., and Fedorov, A., 2011, Effects of ice content on the thermal erosion of permafrost—Implications for coastal and fluvial erosion: Permafrost and Periglacial Processes, v. 22, no. 2, p. 179–187.**

This paper considers the relative importance of thaw versus ablation in eroding frozen, non-cohesive riverbanks using mathematical models and laboratory experiments. The experimental results of the authors can be matched by a purely ablational model above a critical ice content threshold (depending on the Reynolds number of the water). Below this threshold, sediments will thaw, but may or may not move depending on the erosive power of the water and the strength of the medium. The main factor controlling thermal erosion is usually water temperature, as opposed to ground temperature. This model may explain the apparently contradictory field observations of erosion potential of the banks of the Lena River.

30. **Eisner, W. R., and Peterson, K. M., 1998, High-resolution pollen analysis of tundra polygons from the North Slope of Alaska: Journal of Geophysical Research, v. 103, no. D22, p. 28929–28937.**

This paper uses palynology along a transect of ice-wedge polygon centers adjacent to the Meade River near the village of Atqasuk, Alaska. The authors showed the ability of pollen analysis to detect long- and short-term changes in vegetation associated with climate as well as landscape change.

31. **Fedorov, A., and Konstantinov, P., 2003, Observations of surface dynamics with thermokarst initiation, Yukechi site, Central Yakutia, *in* Proceedings of the Eighth International Conference on Permafrost, July 21–25, 2003, Zurich, Switzerland, p. 239–243.**

This paper summarizes thermokarst activity and rates of permafrost thaw and subsidence for ice-rich, flat, inter-alas meadows and shallow thermokarst depressions near Yakutsk, Siberia from 1992 to 2001. In the years of monitoring, the bottom of thermokarst lakes in the area deepened and expanded and separate lakes joined together. Before the authors' observations, the studied sites had maintained their original shapes for 50 years. Intense warming during the 1990s and the high ice content of the soils in the area may explain the observed rapid changes. Surface subsidence on flat areas from 1993 to 2001 was 7–8 cm, and up to 14–15 cm on the edges of small thaw lakes. Surface subsidence may not always be correlated with individual elements of climate, but, rather, multiple factors acting together may either enhance or inhibit thawing and thermokarst formation. For example, in 1998, there were high summer temperatures in Yakutia, but these temperatures did not affect subsidence, which could be explained by enhanced biota productivity. An index of larch tree-ring growth for that year was 43 percent higher than the long-term norm.

32. **Fortier, D., Allard, M., and Shur, Y., 2007, Observation of rapid drainage system development by thermal erosion of ice wedges on Bylot Island, Canadian Arctic Archipelago: Permafrost and Periglacial Processes, v. 18, no. 3, p. 229–243.**
This paper describes the rapid development of a 750-m-long drainage system through the process of thermal erosion of ice wedges over a 4-year period on Bylot Island, Canada. The gully system was created by the formation of sinkholes in ice wedges, which resulted from water flowing through open frost cracks. The sinkholes evolved into underground tunnels that subsequently widened and led to the collapse of the overlying roof of tundra peat and vegetation. Over the 4-year period, open gully headwalls retreated at a mean rate of 15.5 m/yr with maximum rates of about 5 m/d following snowmelt and subsequent runoff. The drainage gully stabilized after a period of 4 years. Development of this new drainage network affected the local hydrology of the hillslope in which it formed. Towards the end of the thaw season, the gully system provided a channel in which to route drainage from the active layer, melting ice wedges, and thawing permafrost to the proglacial river at the base of the slope. Further studies on a regional scale are recommended to assess whether these features and processes are widespread or the result of rare local factors encountered on Bylot Island.

33. **Francis, J.A., White, D.M., Cassano, J.J., Gutowski Jr., W.J., Hinzman, L.D., Holland, M.M., Steele, M.A., and Vörösmarty, C.J,. 2009, An arctic hydrologic system in transition—Feedbacks and impacts on terrestrial, marine, and human life: Journal of Geophysical Research, v. 114, no. G4, G04019.**
This paper divides the arctic hydrologic system into interrelated components and heuristically (that is, graphically) shows their relationship with the biological system (marine and terrestrial). The paper also shows feedback loops and visually assesses the arctic hydrologic system in a seasonally ice free state. Specifically, the hydrologic system was divided into subsystems emphasizing interactions that occur primarily within the atmospheric, oceanic, terrestrial, or global systems. Hydrological subsystems include factors such as cloud cover, total column water vapor, surface air temperature, annual-mean net precipitation, and sea-ice thickness and area. Biological subsystems include human well-being, marine primary productivity, and land cover-ecosystem-vegetation. The paper found that the atmosphere drives much of the arctic hydrological cycle, both directly through net precipitation and indirectly through energy-transfer processes that affect the surface. Furthermore, at least three of these subsystems have changed demonstrably since the 1970s, affecting all components of the system. The paper also provides tables of the overall effect (with direction) of each physical feedback on a biological component of the system. Some notable relationships include possible increases in nutrients to coastal water and marine productivity resulting from freshwater runoff from land but also increases in surface stratification, which reduces mixing of nutrients from below. Similarly, increased surface freshwater increases stratification, which keeps organisms near light sources but blocks upwelling of nutrients from deeper layers. Warmer air temperatures will benefit some species of phytoplankton and zooplankton and reduce others.

34. **French, H.M., 1974, Active thermokarst processes, eastern Banks Island, western Canadian arctic: Canadian Journal of Earth Sciences, v. 11, no. 6, p. 785–794.**
This paper describes various active thermokarst processes occurring on Banks Island in the western Canadian Arctic, a region underlain by ice-rich glacial silt, sand, and gravel. The primary features in this area are ground-ice slumps (thaw slumps). The mean retreat rate of thaw slump headwalls was observed at between 8 and 10 cm/d and, assuming a duration of 75 days in the thaw season, maximum retreat rates of 6 to 8 m/yr were possible. Initiation of the thaw slumps is thought to result from local geomorphic factors, together with rapid thermal erosion along ice wedges. The headwall retreat rate primarily was a function of ground-ice content, and the ultimate stabilization of the slump was related to the balance between the rate at which debris is supplied to, and removed from, the base of the headwall. Based on these estimated rates of retreat and analysis of slumps in aerial photographs, the author speculated that the slumps likely stabilize in 30 to 50 years after their initiation.

35. **French, H.M., 1975, Man-induced thermokarst, Sachs Harbour Airstrip, Banks Island, Northwest Territories: Canadian Journal of Earth Sciences, v. 12, no. 2, p. 132–144.**
This paper describes the degradation of ice wedges associated with the installation of an airstrip on Banks Island, Canada. The silts, sands, and gravel that underlie the surface are ice-rich, with values ranging from 20 to 95percent excess ice content. Degradation of ice wedges and development of thermokarst occurred rapidly in the first 3 years following construction of the airstrip, and subsidence of about 10 cm was measured using survey equipment. Repeat surveys at the site in the first decade following disturbance indicated that thermokarst is still progressing actively at the site. In one summer, a 22-m-long gully formed that bisected the airstrip.

36. **French, H., and Shur, Y., 2010, The principles of cryostratigraphy: Earth-Science Reviews, v. 101, no. 3, p. 190–206.**
This paper provides background information related to the field of cryostratigraphy, which adopts concepts from Russian geocryology as well as modern sedimentology. The primary objective of cryostratigraphy is to provide information on the genesis of perennially frozen sediments. Various layers or distinct zones in permafrost can be distinguished as being representative of different cryostructures. Cryostructures are defined as structures formed by the amount and distribution of ice within sediment and rock. Information on cryostructures is essential for determining the amount of potential thaw settlement at a given site and the likelihood of thermokarst formation. A schematic of the North American cryostructure classification system is shown in figure 5 of the paper.

37. **Frey, K.E., and McClelland, J.W., 2009, Impacts of permafrost degradation on arctic river biogeochemistry: Hydrological Processes, v. 23, no. 1, p. 169–182.**
This paper presents a review of studies linking permafrost dynamics to river biogeochemistry. An overarching theme is that these systems may evolve from surface water- to groundwater-dominated systems as permafrost thaws. This likely will have consequences for solute and nutrient delivery; however, there is little consensus on how river solute concentrations will change. There also are uncertainties in the magnitude of these changes because we are unable to accurately predict how river hydrographs will change in the future. Little consideration is given to the effect of increased river loads on aquatic biogeochemistry, except to say that, as more nitrogen and phosphorus are leached from previously frozen mineral soils, primary productivity may be bolstered.

38. **Frohn, R.C., Hinkel, K.M., and Eisner, W.R., 2005, Satellite remote sensing classification of thaw lakes and drained thaw-lake basins on the North Slope of Alaska: Remote Sensing of Environment, v. 97, no. 1, p. 116–126.**
This paper demonstrates a technique for mapping thermokarst lakes and drained lake basins on the North Slope of Alaska using Landsat satellite imagery and an object-oriented classification algorithm. Classification accuracy for identifying lakes and basins was greater than 93 percent. The end result was a map showing that the western Arctic Coastal Plain was covered with 20 percent lakes and 25 percent drained basins.

39. **Gooseff, M.N., Balser, A., Bowden, W.B., and Jones, J.B., 2009, Effects of hillslope thermokarst in northern Alaska: Eos, Transactions American Geophysical Union, v. 90, no. 4, p. 29–36.**
This paper describes the possible physical, chemical, and biological changes as a result of hillslope thermokarst in areas of continuous and discontinuous permafrost. Possible changes include increased sediment and nutrient loading into streams and rivers and changes in vegetation composition near affected areas. Hillslope thermokarst, or thawing of permafrost on hillslopes, results in the failure and mass wasting (downslope movement) of overlying soil and vegetation. Recent hillslope features observed include active layer detachments, thermokarst gullies, and retrogressive thaw slumps. Hillslope thermokarst events are increasing, and remote sensing and aerial photographs suggest that, in some areas of the Arctic Coastal Plain, a greater than 200-percent increase in hillslope permafrost failures has occurred since the 1980s.

40. **Grenier, C., Régnier, D., Mouche, E., Benabderrahmane, H., Costard, F., and Davy, P., 2013, Impact of permafrost development on groundwater flow patterns—A numerical study considering freezing cycles on a two-dimensional vertical cut through a generic river-plain system: Hydrogeology Journal, v. 21, no. 1, p. 257–270.**
This paper used a coupled water and heat flux model to consider the importance of advective flux to talik closure associated with a future glacial maximum. The study concerns a deep, alluvial basin in Europe, and shows that advective transport of heat through the subsurface prevents talik closure. This may be applicable to several settings on the Arctic Coastal Plain, including near-stream environments, deep connections between thaw lakes, and, sometime in the future, the duration of subsurface connections through an open talik network.

41. **Grosse, G., Harden, J., Turetsky, M., McGuire, A.D., Camill, P., Tarnocai, C., Frolking, S., Schuur, E.A.G., Jorgenson, M.T., Marchenko, S., Romanovsky, V.E., Wickland, K.P., French, N., Waldrop, M., Bourgeau-Chavez, L., and Striegl, R.G., 2011, Vulnerability of high-latitude soil organic carbon in North America to disturbance: Journal of Geophysical Research, v. 116, no. G4, G00K06.**
Although the authors focus on the vulnerability of soil organic carbon, important thermokarst and thermo-erosion processes are summarized and their effects on soils and ecosystem characteristics are described. The authors quantify areas of 73,000 km^2 and 814,000 km^2 with Cryosols underlain by ice-rich permafrost in Alaska and Canada, respectively. Pulse disturbances affecting soils as rapid processes such as thermokarst, thermo-erosion, and wildfires are defined and differentiated from press disturbances representing more gradual changes such as slow active layer deepening or changes in soil wetness. Approaches for predicting soil and soil carbon changes owing to such disturbances are shown and research and data gaps also are highlighted.

42. **Grosse, G., Jones, B.M., and Arp, C.D., 2013, Thermokarst lakes, drainage, and drained basins, *in* Shroder, J.F., and others, eds., Treatise on geomorphology, v. 8: San Diego, Academic Press, p. 325–353.**

The authors summarize the literature on thermokarst lake dynamics, particularly how they form, their panarctic distribution, and their morphometric, physical, and hydrological characteristics and dynamics. Additionally, thermokarst lake drainage is highlighted as an important process in the thermokarst lake cycle of many lake-rich permafrost landscapes. Processes that may result in drainage and that occur after drainage in basins are defined. A new map of potential thermokarst lake distribution in the Arctic and a map of lake orientation are presented.

43. **Grosse G., Romanovsky V.E., Nelson F.E., Brown, J., and Lewkowicz, A.G., 2010, Why permafrost is thawing, not melting: Eos, Transactions American Geophysical Union, v. 91, no. 9, p. 87.**

The authors highlight the importance of terminology when describing the process of permafrost thaw. In the literature, the incorrect phrase–"melting permafrost" –often is used. The correct terminology is "thawing permafrost". "Melting" describes a phase transition from solid to liquid, which is the case for melting ground ice. However, because permafrost usually is composed of a mixture of ground ice, sediments, organic matter, and other materials, it does not melt entirely (become a liquid). The correct term– "thaw" –describes the transition from below 0°C to above 0°C.

44. **Grosse, G., Romanovsky, V., Walter, K., Morgenstern, A., Lantuit, H., and Zimov, S., 2008, Distribution of thermokarst lakes and ponds at three yedoma sites in Siberia, *in* Proceedings of the Ninth International Conference on Permafrost, June 2008, Fairbanks, AK, p. 551–556.**

The authors of this paper present a GIS-based analysis of lake extraction from three thermokarst lake sites in North Siberia using high-resolution SPOT and Ikonos satellite imagery. The authors found a dramatic difference between their high-resolution lake-derived data layer and global and regional estimates of lake surface area in their study regions. At all three study sites, small and medium sized lakes were abundant but missing in global lake databases. Between 21 and 82 percent of the total lake area in three of the study regions was missing. The authors suggest that these findings have implications for upscaling biogeochemical processes associated with small water bodies, that is, thermokarst ponds and lakes in lake-rich permafrost regions.

45. **Grosse, G., Schirrmeister, L., Kunitsky, V.V., and Hubberten, H.W., 2005, The use of CORONA images in remote sensing of periglacial geomorphology—An illustration from the NE Siberian coast: Permafrost and Periglacial Processes, v. 16, no. 2, p. 163–172.**

This paper describes the use of high-resolution, declassified satellite photography from the U.S. CORONA program (1963–1980) for mapping periglacial landforms in a 250-km^2 area in northeastern Siberia. Imagery resolution in this program ranged from 0.6 to 150 m; however, this paper focused on images with a resolution of about 2. The authors were able to map lakes, depressions, lagoons, gullies, slumps, and pingos using a combination of automated and manual mapping techniques. The use of the CORONA imagery for the Bykovsky Peninsula in northeastern Siberia showed that more than 50 percent of the area had been affected by thermokarst processes during the Holocene.

46. **Grosse, G., Schirrmeister, L., and Malthus, T.J., 2006, Application of Landsat-7 satellite data and a DEM for the quantification of thermokarst-affected terrain types in the periglacial Lena–Anabar coastal lowland: Polar Research, v. 25, no. 1, p. 51–67.**
This paper describes the use of Landsat-7 satellite data and a digital elevation model for the quantification and description of an approximately 3,500-km^2 thermokarst-affected region in northern Siberia. A supervised classification approach was used to determine various thermokarst landforms that relied primarily on relief forms and the spectral response of various tundra vegetation types. The final terrain type classification was composed of eight major classes (seven land classes and one water class). These were divided into 37 subclasses, and the class composition for some of these subclasses was categorized based on thermokarst depressions, pingos, river valleys, thermo-erosional valleys, and yedoma uplands. Thirteen surface classes ultimately were determined to provide good overall classification accuracy (79 percent), and that 78 percent of the study area was affected somewhat by thermokarst, thermo-erosion, and related slope processes.

47. **Harris, C., and Lewkowicz, A.G., 2000, An analysis of the stability of thawing slopes, Ellesmere Island, Nunavut, Canada: Canadian Geotechnical Journal, v. 37, no. 2, p. 449–462.**
This paper examined the potential for failure of two slopes showing evidence of previous active layer detachment slides. Theoretically, detachment failures depend on soil and pore pressures. By measuring soil pore pressure and active layer depths, the authors were able to calculate the safety factor for the given slopes, and to estimate the pore pressures needed to facilitate a detachment slide. Although the tested slopes were in relatively safe states, changes necessary to induce slides were calculated. Depth of saturation and buried sand layers were recognized as two potentially important factors. Shear strength was identified as the most sensitive parameter controlling slope stability; shear strength may decrease annually when active layers are deep, eventually weakening the soils and allowing slides to occur.

48. **Harris, S.A., 2002, Causes and consequences of rapid thermokarst development in permafrost or glacial terrain: Permafrost and Periglacial Processes, v. 13, no. 3, p. 237–242.**
This paper compares air, soil, and water temperature at one location to show that heat is adsorbed differently by soils and water. A lag time between water temperature and ground temperature was observed, and a large disconnect during cooling was noted when winter temperatures reached -3°C and -19°C in the lake and the ground, respectively. The subsurface inflows could have affected the comparison. Discussion focuses on the major differences between soil and water, including heat capacity, thermal diffusivity, and thermal conductivity. Translucency and convection are two important factors that are unique to water and heat storage and exchange. The discussion notes how the differences in thermal properties of water and soils may lead to thermokarst development and shows photographs representing the formation of an alas valley.

49. **Helbig, M., Boike, J., Langer, M., Schreiber, P., Runkle, B.R., and Kutzbach, L., 2013, Spatial and seasonal variability of polygonal tundra water balance—Lena River Delta, northern Siberia (Russia): Hydrogeology Journal, v. 21, no. 1, p. 133–147.**
This paper quantifies the water balance for a polygonal landscape. Besides the obvious and large vertical fluxes (precipitation and evapotranspiration), lateral fluxes are important, especially if polygonal rims and trough margins have degraded because of permafrost thaw. Early-summer snowmelt is an important source of water, and later in the summer, high hydraulic conductivity allows increased subsurface flow. The importance of soil stratification, with higher flow potential in the shallow organic layers, is also recognized.

50. **Hinkel, K.M., Eisner, W.R., Bockheim, J.G., Nelson, F.E., Peterson, K.M., and Dai, X., 2003, Spatial extent, age, and carbon stocks in drained thaw lake basins on the Barrow Peninsula, Alaska: Arctic, Antarctic, and Alpine Research, v. 35, no. 3, p. 291–300.**
This paper estimates the age of 77 drained thaw-lake basins on the Barrow Peninsula based on a predictable succession of plant communities, landscape wetness and texture, and soil organic matter thickness. Field-based classifications were used to categorize four basin types: young, medium, old, and ancient. These determinations were supported by radiocarbon dating of material from the base of the organic layer. Landsat-7 imagery also was used to investigate the potential for classifying lakes based solely on imagery. Core samples indicated that organic layer thickness and degree of decomposition increases with basin age, but there was significant scatter related to cryoturbation, decomposition, and processes leading to ice enrichment in the shallow permafrost.

51. **Hinkel, K.M., Frohn, R.C., Nelson, F.E., Eisner, W.R., and Beck, R.A., 2005, Morphometric and spatial analysis of thaw lakes and drained thaw lake basins in the western Arctic Coastal Plain, Alaska: Permafrost and Periglacial Processes, v. 16, no. 4, p. 327–341.**
Remote sensing data was examined across the western Arctic Coastal Plain, Alaska, to analyze the characteristics of permafrost thaw lakes and drained basins in three subregions that were demarcated by ancient shorelines. Subregions varied by surface age, with older subregions farther than younger subregions from the ca. 2000 coastline. All subregions had similar lake and basin orientation, suggesting summer wind direction has remained relatively constant for several thousand years. Lake coverage (percentage of area) also was similar among subregions, while drained lake basin area decreased in older surfaces. An apparent tradeoff existed between lake and basin size, and density and age of the features: older surfaces contained more, but smaller, lakes and basins than younger surfaces. Many factors may influence lake morphometry, including ground-ice content, surficial sediments, local relief, distance from the coast, and surface age.

52. Hinkel, K.M., and Hurd, J.K., 2006, Permafrost destabilization and thermokarst following snow fence installation, Barrow, Alaska, USA: Arctic, Antarctic, and Alpine Research, v. 38, no. 4, p. 530–539.

This paper describes the effect of a snow fence on permafrost temperature and land subsidence in Barrow, Alaska, from 1999 to 2005. Data loggers were installed at depths of 5, 30, and 50 cm in the ground on the downwind side of the snow fence and in tundra sites not affected by the snow drifts that formed as a result of the snow fence. Active layer thickness and snow depth were measured annually in August and April, respectively. As a result of the snow fence, the ground temperature in the downwind strip has warmed by 2–14°C in the winter, and has cooled by 2–3°C in the summer because of the time it takes to melt the drifted snow (3–4 m in thickness). The net effect has been a warming of the ground surface, a thawing of the permafrost, subsidence of about 10–20 cm, and development of thermokarst ponds. This study highlights the importance of snow accumulation and thickness on the ground thermal regime and potential to form thermokarst in areas where air temperatures are thought to be too cold for the formation of thermokarst.

53. Hinkel, K.M., Jones, B.M., Eisner, W.R., Cuomo, C.J., Beck, R.A., and Frohn, R., 2007, Methods to assess natural and anthropogenic thaw lake drainage on the western Arctic coastal plain of northern Alaska: Journal of Geophysical Research, v. 112, no. F2, F02S16.

This paper describes three methods for assessing the natural and anthropogenic drainage of thermokarst lakes on the western Arctic Coastal Plain of northern Alaska: (1) comparison of Landsat imagery between about 1970 and about 2000 for a 35,000-km^2 area, (2) comparison of historical aerial photography from 1949 to 1955 with recent high-resolution orthorectified radar derived imagery from 2002 for the Barrow Peninsula, and (3) interviews with local and traditional knowledge holders. About 50 lakes larger than 10 ha drained in the 25-year period were analyzed with an automated classification of the Landsat imagery. This analysis showed that only 0.027 percent of the extant lakes in the region had catastrophic drainage during this time period. The authors also attempted to classify the lake drainage events by a mechanism that included lake coalescence (19), coastal erosion (1), stream meandering (8), headward erosion (13), and unresolvable (9). By extending the analysis back to 1950 with the automated classification of the aerial photography for the Barrow study region the authors showed that human activity was responsible for about 40 percent of the lake drainage events on the Barrow Peninsula. The timing and mechanism of select lake drainage events were further refined through the interviews with the traditional and local knowledge holders.

54. Hinkel, K.M., Lenters, J.D., Sheng, Y., Lyons, E.A., Beck, R.A., Eisner, W.R., Maurer, E.F., Wang, J., and Potter, B.L., 2012, Thermokarst lakes on the Arctic Coastal Plain of Alaska—Spatial and temporal variability in summer water temperature: Permafrost and Periglacial Processes, v. 23, p. 207–217.

This paper describes the rate of water warming throughout the summer and spatial variation in water temperature across the Arctic Coastal Plain, Alaska. During the summer of 2010, vertical water temperature measurements were collected in 12 thermokarst lakes across this plain. Water temperature was measured using sensor strings affixed to nylon rope with a float or weight at the end placed in lakes before or during ice decay. Water warming in the spring begins at the lakebed during ice decay. Temperatures rapidly increase after ice-off and correspond to local weather conditions. Ice-off occurs 2–4 weeks later on lakes near the coast, and coastal lakes are an average of 6°C cooler than inland lakes. Lakes are well mixed and mostly isothermal; the average mean bottom water temperature for lakes 1.0–3.5-m deep is 0.1–0.5°C cooler than that of near-surface water. A series of detailed measurements over a short time period on a single lake showed warmer (2–3°C) temperatures on the upwind, sheltered end of the lake. These data can be used to calibrate high-resolution satellite thermal bands and to develop classification methods to characterize thermokarst lakes according to water temperature.

55. Hinkel, K.M., Sheng, Y., Lenters, J.D., Lyons, E.A., Beck, R.A., Eisner, W.R., and Wang, J., 2012, Thermokarst lakes on the Arctic Coastal Plain of Alaska—Geomorphic controls on bathymetry: Permafrost and Periglacial Processes, v. 23, p. 218–230.

This study summarizes the bathymetry of thermokarst lakes across the Arctic Coastal Plain, Alaska, in relation to surficial sediments (that is, soil types) and topography. Lake sensors were used to estimate water depth and GPS-enabled sonar was used to collect detailed bathymetric data during the summer months of 2008–2010. Lake depth varied with nearness to the coast. Coastal lowland lakes that developed in marine silts tended to be shallow (about 2 m deep) and of more uniform depth. Farther inland, lakes formed in ice-poor Aeolian sand deposits and generally were about 1-m deep, but had deeper central pools (2–5 m deep). Lakes in the Arctic Coastal Plain-Arctic Foothills transition zone developed in loess uplands and were extremely ice-rich. Residual lakes inside old lake basins generally were uniformly 2–4 m deep, but at times contained deeper (6–9 m deep) pools where the expanding lake encroached on uplands at eroding bluffs. The authors speculate these deeper pools were formed by ground subsidence from thawing ice-rich permafrost above ice wedges. The data presented can be used to develop and calibrate models with high-resolution passive or active remote sensing systems to estimate water depth. Coarse spatial resolution of the data restricts the ability to detect deep pools and steep gradients. This need to incorporate sediment erosion and transport in bathymetry models of thermokarst lakes is also highlighted in the study.

56. Hopkins, D.M., 1949, Thaw lakes and thaw sinks in the Imuruk Lake area, Seward Peninsula, Alaska: The Journal of Geology, p. 119–131.

This paper describes thermokarst lakes and sinks (depressions left after lakes drain subterraineously) in the Imuruk Lake area on the Seward Peninsula of Alaska. The region contains frozen, silty soils with ground ice with natural porosity greater than that of the potentially unfrozen material. The melting of this ice leads to land subsidence and ponding of water in the depressions that further promote thaw. Early English definitions are given for (1) thaw depressions–depressions that result from the subsidence following the thawing of permafrost; (2) thaw (thermokarst) lakes–lakes that occupy thaw depressions, including lakes that originated in other ways but that have been enlarged considerably by thawing at their margins; and (3) thaw sinks closed depressions with a subterranean drainage but believed to have originated as thermokarst lakes. Thermokarst lakes in the region were formed by many different processes: (1) disruption of the vegetal cover by frost heaving, (2) accelerated thaw beneath pools at the intersection of ice wedges, and (3) accelerated thaw beneath pools in small streams. Wave erosion becomes an important enlargement process when a waterbody is larger than about 30 m in diameter. Although the average expansion rates of lakes are not provided in the study, some of the faster rates of lake expansion ever recorded in the Arctic (more than 20 m/yr during a 2-yr period) were noted.

57. Johnson, C.J., Boyce, M.S., Mulders, R., Gunn, A., Gau, R.J., Cluff, H.D., and Case, R.L., 2004, Quantifying patch distribution at multiple spatial scales—Applications to wildlife-habitat models: Landscape Ecology, v. 19, no. 8, p. 869–882.

This paper describes an approach for examining habitat relationships for three arctic mammals in the Canadian central Arctic: gray wolf, brown bear, and caribou. A technique was used that quantifies habitat at the patch scale and the distribution of multiple patches (that is, patch density) at a larger regional scale. Most conservative models for wolves and grizzly bears included characteristics at both spatial scales, but caribou were best described using only regional-scale characteristics. Caribou during the post-calving season preferred many small patches of lichen veneer, heath tundra, and rocks in a region. During denning, wolves preferred heath rock and heath tundra as well as patches of sedge, lichen veneer, and rock. Resource selection by grizzly bears during early summer was best explained by esker (sparsely vegetated sand and gravel ridges) and low shrub, and a low density of forest and sedge patches. Integration of environmental characteristics at multiple scales was recommended when monitoring mobile animals that range across heterogeneous areas.

58. Jones, B.M., Arp, C.D., Jorgenson, M.T., Hinkel, K.M., Schmutz, J.A., and Flint, P.L., 2009, Increase in the rate and uniformity of coastline erosion in Arctic Alaska: Geophysical Research Letters, v. 36, no. 3, L03503.

This study compares aerial photography along a 60-km stretch of the Beaufort Sea coastline from 1955, 1979, 2002, and 2007. The authors determined that erosion rates increased from 6.8 m/yr to 8.7 m/yr to 13.6 m/yr, respectively. The rate of erosion along coastal areas with varying degrees of ice-richness became more similar over time, possibly indicating that thermal erosion had increased along this stretch of coast.

59. **Jones, B.M., Grosse, G., Arp, C.D., Jones, M.C., Anthony, K.W., and Romanovsky, V.E., 2011, Modern thermokarst lake dynamics in the continuous permafrost zone, northern Seward Peninsula, Alaska: Journal of Geophysical Research, v. 116, no. G2, G00M03.**

This paper describes the expansion and drainage of thermokarst lakes for a 700-km^2 area on the northern Seward Peninsula of Alaska between 1950 and 2007. The authors compared the surface area of lakes selected from aerial photography acquired in about 1950 and 1978, and a high-resolution satellite image acquired in 2006 and 2007. Lakes larger than 0.1 ha were selected from each image set using an object-oriented classification algorithm and were manually adjusted where necessary. The number of waterbodies increased by 10 percent during the study period, but the total surface area associated with the waterbodies decreased by 15 percent. These changes primarily resulted from the partial drainage of several large lakes and the formation of remnant ponds. Lakes larger than 40 ha decreased in number by 24- percent and in surface area by 26- percent. One likely factor responsible for lake drainage was the expansion of lakes towards a drainage gradient. Thermokarst lake expansion rates, based on analysis of about 400 waterbodies, averaged about 0.35 m/yr with maximum rates of almost 6 m/yr. Thermokarst lake expansion rates were higher for lower bluffs (0.4 m/yr) than for higher bluffs (0.2 m/yr) associated with yedoma terrain. Lake drainage rates during the study period were 2.2 lakes per year. These findings have implications at the landscape scale, as nearly three times more land area was gained relative to land area lost through thermokarst lake dynamics during the study period.

60. **Jones, B.M., Grosse, G., Hinkel, K.M., Arp, C.D., Walker, S., Beck, R.A., and Galloway, J.P., 2012, Assessment of pingo distribution and morphometry using an IfSAR derived digital surface model, western Arctic Coastal Plain, northern Alaska: Geomorphology, 138, v. 1, p. 1–14.**

This paper mapped the distribution and morphometry of pingos in a 40,000-km^2 area on the western Arctic Coastal Plain of northern Alaska using a digital surface model from about 2005 derived from airborne Interferometric Synthetic Aperture Radar (IfSAR). The authors identified 1,247 pingo-like features between 2 and 21 m high, 400 more than previously were mapped in the region. The highest pingo density (0.18/km^2) occurred where streams had reworked aeolian sand deposits. Morphometric analyses indicated that most pingos were small-to-medium in size (less than200 m in diameter), gently-to-moderately sloping (less than30°), circular–to-slightly elongate (mean circularity index of 0.88), and of relatively low height (2–5 m). However, 57 pingos were higher than 10 m, 26 had a maximum slope of greater than 30°, and 42 were larger than 200 m in diameter. Comparing the 2005-derived pingo dataset with the pingo dataset created from mid-1950s stereo-pair aerial photography, 66 pingos may have partially or completely collapsed during the 50-year period. Only two pingos were positively identified as having formed over the same period. However, caution should be taken when comparing contemporary and legacy datasets derived using different techniques.

61. **Jorgenson, M.T., 2011, Coastal region of northern Alaska, Guidebook to permafrost and related features; Alaska Division of Geological and Geophysical Surveys, Guidebook 10, p. 188.**

This guidebook and overview of northern Alaska was developed during the Ninth International Conference on Permafrost, held in Fairbanks, Alaska, in 2008. It is organized into five sections. The first section provides an overview of the Arctic Coastal Plain with an emphasis on the role of permafrost in shaping ecological and social systems. The second section provides an overview of oil development in the region, and the remaining three sections provide information on field trips taken to the Prudhoe Bay and Kuparuk oilfields, the Colville River Delta, and the Barrow Peninsula.

62. **Jorgenson, M.T., 2013, Thermokarst terrains *in* Shroder, J.F, and others, eds., Treatise on geomorphology, v. 8: San Diego, Academic Press, p. 313–324.**

This book chapter provides an overview of 23 thermokarst landforms associated with varying terrain conditions, ground ice volumes and morphologies, and heat and mass transfer processes that have been identified in Arctic, Subarctic, and Antarctic regions. These features include (1) deep thermokarst lake, (2) shallow thermokarst lake, (3) glacial thermokarst lake, (4) glacial thermokarst, (5) thermokarst basin, (6) thermokarst lake basin, (7) thaw sink, (8) thermokarst fen, (9) thermokarst bog, (10) thermokarst shore fen, (11) thaw slump, (12) detachment slide, (13) collapsed pingo, (14) beaded stream, (15) thermal erosion gully, (16) thermokarst water track, (17) collapse-block shore, (18) ice-block landslide, (19) thermokarst troughs and pits, (20) thermokarst pits, (21) conical thermokarst mounds, (22) irregular thermokarst mounds, and (23) sink holes. The chapter focuses on (1) describing the nature of various landforms; (2) identifying the dominant processes and stages involved in permafrost degradation; and (3) discussing the climatic and terrain factors affecting regional and local thermokarst. An overview on thermokarst landforms, typical feature size, mass transfer process, heat source, hydrologic regime, dominant ice type, depth of subsidence, and lateral rate of expansion is given in table 1 of the chapter.

63. **Jorgenson, M.T., and Osterkamp, T.E., 2005, Response of boreal ecosystems to varying modes of permafrost degradation: Canadian Journal of Forest Research, v. 35, no. 9, p. 2100–2111.**

This paper provides an overview of 16 primary modes of surface permafrost degradation based on their microtopography and vegetative characteristics for the boreal forest region of Alaska. The mode of permafrost degradation or type of thermokarst is highly variable, and its topographic and ecological consequences depend on the interaction of slope position, soil texture, hydrology, and ice content. The 16 modes identified in the paper include: (1) thermokarst lakes from lateral thermo-mechanical erosion, (2) thermokarst basins after lake drainage, (3) thaw sinks from subsurface drainage of lakes, (4) glacial thermokarst of ice-cored moraines, (5) linear collapse-scar fens associated with shallow groundwater movement, (6) round isolated collapse-scar bogs from slow lateral degradation, (7) small round isolated thermokarst pits from surface thawing, (8) polygonal thermokarst mounds from advanced ice-wedge degradation, (9) mixed thermokarst pits and polygons from initial ice-wedge degradation, (10) irregular thermokarst mounds from thawing of ice-poor silty soils, (11) sinkholes and pipes resulting from groundwater flow, (12) thermokarst gullies and water tracks from surface-water flow, (13) thaw slumps related to slope failure and thawing, (14) thermo-erosional niches from water undercutting of ice-rich shores, (15) collapsed pingos from thawing of massive ice in pingos, and (16) non-patterned ground from thawing of ice-poor soils. Information on each degradation mode related to landscape position, hydrologic regime, soil texture, excess ice content, dominant ice morphology, typical size, thaw settlement, and later degradation rate is given in table 1 of this paper. The various degradation modes lead to very different ecological responses, ranging from the creation of new lakes and aquatic habitat to conversion of forests to fen and bog meadows. Although the focus of this paper is on boreal ecosystems, many of the modes occur in the Arctic as well.

64. **Jorgenson, M.T., Racine, C.H., Walters, J.C., and Osterkamp, T.E., 2001, Permafrost degradation and ecological changes associated with a warming climate in central Alaska: Climatic change, v. 48, no. 4, p. 551–579.**

This paper presents studies from 1994–1998 on the Tanana Flats in central Alaska that reveal that permafrost degradation is widespread and rapid, causing large shifts in ecosystems from birch forests to fens and bogs. Fine-grained soils under the birch forest are ice-rich and thaw settlement is typically 1–2.5 m after the permafrost thaws. The collapsed areas are rapidly colonized by aquatic herbaceous plants, leading to the development of a thick, floating organic mat. Based on field sampling of soils, permafrost and vegetation, and the construction of a GIS database, an estimated 17 percent of the study area (263,964 ha) was unfrozen with no previous permafrost, 48 percent had stable permafrost, 31 percent was partially degraded, and 4 percent was totally degraded. For that part of the study area that currently has, or recently had, permafrost (83 percent of the area), about 42 percent was affected by thermokarst development. Based on aerial photograph analysis, birch forests decreased by 35 percent and fens increased by 29 percent from 1949 to 1995. Overall, the area with totally degraded permafrost (collapse-scar fens and bogs) has increased from 39 to 47 percent in 46 years. Based on rates of change from airphoto analysis and radiocarbon dating, an estimated 83 percent of the degradation occurred before 1949. Evidence indicates that this permafrost degradation began in the mid-1700s and is associated with relatively warm climatic periods during the mid-to-late 1700s and the 1900s. If current conditions persist, the remaining lowland birch forests will disappear by the end of the next century.

65. **Jorgenson, M.T., Romanovsky, V., Harden, J., Shur, Y., O'Donnell, J., Schuur, E.A., Kanevskiy, M., and Marchenko, S., 2010, Resilience and vulnerability of permafrost to climate change, *in* The Dynamics of change in Alaska's boreal forests—Resilience and vulnerability in response to climate warming: Canadian Journal of Forest Research, v. 40, no. 7, p. 1219–1236.**

This paper examines the relations among environmental factors that influence permafrost resilience and vulnerability to disturbance through the use of field measurements, numerical modeling, and a literature review. The resilience or vulnerability of permafrost to climate change depends on the complex interaction between topography, water, soil, vegetation, and snow. Changes in surface water atop permafrost were shown to have the greatest effect on permafrost thaw.

66. Jorgenson, M.T., and Shur, Y., 2007, Evolution of lakes and basins in northern Alaska and discussion of the thaw lake cycle: Journal of Geophysical Research, v. 112, no. F2, F02S17.

This paper provides a revision of the thaw-lake cycle on the Arctic Coastal Plain of northern Alaska based on topographic profiles, soil and ground-ice surveys, radiocarbon dating, photogrammetric analysis, and regional comparisons. The primary study area was located on part of the sand sheet deposits west of the Colville River Delta. The authors state that there is not enough ground ice in this surface geology unit to be able to form a thermokarst lake and that most lakes on the Arctic Coastal Plain are of non-thermokarst origin. Formation of most of the Arctic Coastal Plain lakes includes (1) initial flooding of depressions to form primary lakes, (2) lateral erosion, with sorting and redistribution of sediments, (3) lake drainage as the stream network expands, (4) differential ice aggradation in silty centers and sandy margins, (5) formation of secondary thaw lakes in the heaved centers of ice-rich basins and infilling of ponds along the low margins, and (6) basin stabilization. These criteria led to the development of lake classification scheme for the Arctic Coastal Plain that consisted of "true" thaw lakes, depression lakes, riverine lakes, and delta lakes. Shoreline erosion rates were assessed for a small region in what was classified as "depression lakes" however for secondary lakes that formed in the ice-rich centers of drained lake basins. Maximum erosion rates were about 0.8 m/yr; however, mean erosion rates typically were less than 0.1 m/yr. Based on these estimates, the authors asserted that lakes expand too slowly for multiple cycles of formation and drainage to have occurred during the Holocene.

67. Jorgenson, M.T., Shur, Y.L., and Osterkamp, T.E., 2008, Thermokarst in Alaska, *in* Proceedings of the Ninth International Conference on Permafrost, June 2008, Fairbanks, AK, p. 869–76.

This paper provides an overview of thermokarst features in Alaska by classifying and characterizing landforms associated with permafrost degradation, estimating the aerial extent of thermokarst in Alaska, and estimating the rate of degradation in various regions. Twenty thermokarst landforms were identified through a combination of field surveys and aerial photograph analysis that varied in relation to climate, geomorphic environments and soil texture, hydrologic regime, and ice morphology and content: (1) deep and shallow thermokarst lakes, (2) drained thaw-lake basins, (3) thaw-lake sinks, (4) thermokarst pits, (5) thermokarst troughs and pits, (6) collapsed pingos, (7) thermokarst shore bogs, (8) thermokarst bogs and fens, (9) thermokarst gullies, (10) thermokarst water tracks, (11) beaded streams, (12) thaw slumps, (13) detachment slides, (14) sink holes and tunnels, (15) glacial thermokarst, (16) collapse-block shores, (17) block landslides, (18) thermokarst conical mounds, (19) irregular mounds, and (20) non-patterned thawed ground. Information on each landform related to mass transfer, heat source, hydrologic regime, dominant ice type, typical size, settlement, and lateral expansion rate is given in table 1 of this paper. The extent of thermokarst features was assessed through analysis of aerial photographs taken along transects in select regions of the state. Based on this analysis, the authors determined that, in the discontinuous permafrost zone, 61 percent of the area had permafrost and 5 percent of the area constituted thermokarst; whereas, in the continuous permafrost zone, 13.5 percent of the area constituted thermokarst. The authors also assessed the rate of change of thermokarst formation at four sites along a latitudinal gradient in Alaska and determined that area affected increased from 3.5 to 8 percent.

68. Jorgenson, M.T., Shur, Y.L., and Pullman, E.R., 2006, Abrupt increase in permafrost degradation in Arctic Alaska: Geophysical Research Letters, v. 33, no. 2, L02503.
This paper describes the degradation of ice wedges between 1945 and 2001 on part of the Arctic Coastal Plain of northern Alaska west of the Colville River Delta. Ice wedges here are thought to have been stable for thousands of years. Ice-wedge degradation was evaluated at three spatial scales: (1) field surveys at two sites (1.2 km^2), (2) manual change detection with aerial photography at the two intensive sites (1.2 km^2), and (3) automated change detection using spectral characteristics of a larger area in the same region (29 km^2). In the field, ice-wedge degradation was classified into six stages: (1) undegraded ice wedges with no evident surface changes; (2) initial degradation with barely evident settlement associated with thawing of the transient layer and greening of tussocks; (3) intermediate degradation with obvious settlement, shallow standing water, and robust green tussocks; (4) advanced degradation with deep, water-filled pits and dead submerged tussocks; (5) initial stabilization with robust aquatic sedges in shallow water; and (6) advanced stabilization associated with thick peat accumulation, reestablishment of a permafrost layer above the ice wedges, reduction of surface water, and establishment of mosses. In the photography, ice-wedge degradation and stabilization at the two intensive study sites was identified as the region in the study area covered by a water-filled pit. Thermokarst pits increased slowly from 0.5 percent in 1945 to 0.6 percent in 1982, and then increased abruptly to 4.4 percent by 2001. Similarly, pit density (that is, the density of pits with areas greater than 12 m^2) increased slowly from 88/km^2 in 1945 to 128/km^2 in 1982, then rapidly to 1,336/km^2 by 2001. In contrast, the percent area of stabilizing pits showed only gradual changes over the three dates (1.6 percent, 2.2 percent, and 3.0 percent, respectively), as earlier degrading pits became stabilized. The automated classification of the larger area revealed similar patterns. By combining the field studies with the aerial photography, the authors showed that initial and advanced degradation can happen within 20 years and that advanced stabilization occurs within an additional 20–30 years. The authors attributed the abrupt increase in ice-wedge degradation after 1982 to warm summer temperatures between 1989 and 1998; however they did not consider potential increases to winter temperatures nor to increased snowfall. The degradation of ice wedges at the study site has caused a substantial redistribution of surface water from the adjacent tundra. These processes may affect 10–30 percent of the arctic lowland terrestrial landscapes.

69. Jorgenson, M.T., Yoshikawa, K., Kanevskiy, M., Shur, Y., Romanovsky, V., Marchenko, S., Grosse, G., Brown, J., and Jones, B., 2008, Permafrost characteristics of Alaska, *in* Proceedings of the Ninth International Conference on Permafrost, June 2008, Fairbanks, AK, map.

This map is an update to the permafrost distribution map for Alaska using a terrain-unit approach based on climate and surficial geology. It is the third iteration of the statewide map. The permafrost map is coded with information on surficial geology, mean annual air temperature, primary soil texture, permafrost extent, ground ice volume, and primary thermokarst landforms. The main map on p. 1 shows the distribution of continuous, discontinuous, sporadic, and isolated permafrost in Alaska along with locations in which the permafrost thickness is known. On p. 2, there are six accompanying maps that show PRISM-based mean annual air temperature, surface geology, ground temperatures, ground ice, pingos, ice wedges, and thermokarst landforms. The thermokarst landform map shows 13 types of resolvable features at the mapping scale: (1) deep thermokarst lakes, (2) shallow thermokarst lakes, (3) basins, (4) troughs, (5) pits, (6) sinks, (7) bogs, (8) fens, (9) thaw slumps, (10) gullies, (11) water tracks, (12) polygonal troughs, and (13) glacial thermokarst. The authors state that, although this map is an improvement of the prior two mapping efforts, a better surficial geology map is needed with updated information and better spatial accuracy, more information on terrain-ground ice-temperature-permafrost relationships, more temperature boreholes, and improved spatial models.

70. Kanevskiy, M., Shur, Y., Fortier, D., Jorgenson, M.T., and Stephani, E., 2011, Cryostratigraphy of late Pleistocene syngenetic permafrost (yedoma) in northern Alaska, Itkillik River exposure: Quaternary Research, v. 75, no. 3, p. 584–596.

This paper provides an overview on the nature and distribution of yedoma in the Arctic, describes the characteristics of a yedoma exposure in northern Alaska, and provides an overview map of the potential distribution of yedoma in Alaska. Yedoma permafrost deposits typically refer to late-Pleistocene syngenetic permafrost, which typically has very high ground-ice content. The exposure that was studied in northern Alaska represents 40,000 years of undisturbed yedoma formation. The lack of yedoma in certain regions of northern Alaska forms the basis of the hypothesis that parts of the Arctic Coastal Plain were glaciated during the Pleistocene.

71. Kanevskiy, M., Shur, Y., Jorgenson, M.T., Ping, C.L., Michaelson, G.J., Fortier, D., Stephani, E., Dillon, M., and Tumskoy, V., 2013, Ground ice in the upper permafrost of the Beaufort Sea coast of Alaska: Cold Regions Science and Technology, v. 85, p. 56–70.

This paper quantifies ice structures in the five dominant terrain units on the Arctic Coastal Plain: (1) primary surface (silty deposits in the west to gravelly sand in the east), (2) low yedoma foothills, (3) drained lake basins, (4) deltas and tidal flats, and (5) eolian sand dunes. Wedge-ice volumes and total volumetric ice were calculated. Wedge ice was the dominant form of massive ice, ranging from 3 to 50 percent, and occurring in nearly all terrains. Other types of massive ice included thermokarst cave ice, ice core pingos, and folded massive ice. Most of the soils were classified as frost-susceptible silts, resulting in extremely ice-rich permafrost dominated by ataxitic cryostructure. Ice content was notably lower in young drained lake basins, deltas, and tidal flats. The authors discussed formation and calculation of the size of the transition layer, which is the ice-rich upper part of the permafrost, the formation of which greatly elevates the landscape.

72. **Karlsson, J.M., Bring, A., Peterson, G.D., Gordon, L.J., and Destouni, G., 2011, Opportunities and limitations to detect climate-related regime shifts in inland Arctic ecosystems through eco-hydrological monitoring: Environmental Research Letters, v. 6, no. 1, p. 014015.**
This study identifies and maps three climate-driven, hydrologically-mediated regime shifts in inland Arctic ecosystems (1) tundra to shrubland or forest, (2) terrestrial ecosystem to thermokarst lakes and wetlands, and (3) thermokarst lakes and wetlands to terrestrial ecosystems. Areal coverage of these shifts was compared with monitoring data based on a literature review of nearly 200 publications, recognizing the large degree of overlap in the Yukon, Mackenzie, Barents-Norwegian Sea, and Ob Rivers Basins between aerially observed changes and monitoring. Tundra-to-shrubland and terrestrial-to-aquatic regimes were observed to occur in unmonitored areas, and carbon fluxes were observed to be undermonitored compared to nitrogen and phosphorus in areas that are drying. Most regime shifts were occurring in Alaska (67 percent), and a spatial mismatch existed between the locations of hydrological and ecological monitoring.

73. **Kessler, M. A., Plug, L.J., and Anthony, K.W., 2012, Simulating the decadal-to millennial-scale dynamics of morphology and sequestered carbon mobilization of two thermokarst lakes in NW Alaska: Journal of Geophysical Research, v. 117, G00M06.**
This paper uses a three-dimensional numerical model to combine elements of lake evolution, thermokarst thaw, and carbon mobilization to predict methane efflux from two arctic lake basins situated in yedoma permafrost. Lake growth and methane production were highly dependent on topography, indicating the need for high-resolution topographic maps to make accurate predictions. Observed and modeled methane emissions differed by about a factor of 2, with the largest uncertainties in soil carbon content and actual methane emission rates. Both lakes expanded, merged, and drained several times during the simulation, highlighting that methane emissions depend on the expansion of thermokarst thaw lakes into virgin yedoma, not just expansion or refilling

74. **Koch, J.C., Ewing, S.A., Striegl, R., and McKnight, D.M., 2013, Rapid runoff via shallow throughflow and deeper preferential flow in a boreal catchment underlain by frozen silt (Alaska, USA): Hydrogeology Journal, v. 21, no. 1, p. 93–106.**
This paper investigates seasonal changes in runoff lags, ratios, and pathways from a north-facing, continuous permafrost silty hillslope in interior Alaska. This combination of soil moisture data and infiltration modeling indicates the presence of rapid preferential flowpaths that drain the hillslope quickly, even in late summer when soil active layers are greatest. Uranium isotopes indicate that these flows are contacting virgin permafrost, which may occur as streams incise into their beds, and (or) are associated with slumps. This effect may be maximized at this study site because of a recent fire that increased the active layer.

75. **Kokelj, S.V., Jenkins, R.E., Milburn, D., Burn, C.R., and Snow, N. 2005, The influence of thermokarst disturbance on the water quality of small upland lakes, Mackenzie Delta region, Northwest Territories, Canada: Permafrost and Periglacial Processes, v. 16, no. 4, p. 343–353.**
This paper compares lake chemistry between small lakes (area of less than 20 ha; 22 lakes), where half of the lakes are pristine and the other half have been affected by thermokarst. Higher concentrations of major ions and lower concentrations of dissolved organic carbon were noted in the thermokarst lakes. Significant correlations were found between the percentage of the basin affected by thermokarst and lake chemistry. Altered chemistry was

observed in lakes, with as little as 2 percent of the basin affected by thermokarst. These effects persisted for decades after slump development had ceased.

76. **Kokelj, S.V., Lantz, T.C., Kanigan, J., Smith, S.L., and Coutts, R., 2009, Origin and polycyclic behaviour of tundra thaw slumps, Mackenzie Delta region, Northwest Territories, Canada: Permafrost and Periglacial Processes, v. 20, no. 2, p. 173–184.**
This study addresses the effect of retrogressive thaw slumps on tundra landscapes and talik formation. The difference in temperatures on virgin tundra and on retrogressive thaw slump scars was measured, and this information was used to inform a two-dimensional numerical model of heat flow and talik formation in lakes. Simulations were compared to digital aerial photography that had been analyzed to identify slump age and evidence of polycyclic behavior (overlapping slumps of multiple ages). Slumps were determined to greatly increase heat flow into the ground (owing to removal of the surface organic cover) and also to promote winter snow accumulation, which inhibits ground heat loss. Together, these processes act to warm and potentially to thaw permafrost. Feedbacks between slumping, talik enlargement, and thaw subsidence may drive polycyclic retrogressive thaw slumping.

77. **Kokelj, S.V., Zajdlik, B., and Thompson, M.S., 2009, The impacts of thawing permafrost on the chemistry of lakes across the subarctic boreal-tundra transition, Mackenzie Delta region, Canada: Permafrost and Periglacial Processes, v. 20, no. 2, p. 185–199.**
This paper compares lake water chemistry for 39 lakes that have not been affected by thermokarst with 24 lakes that have been affected by thermokarst. Higher concentrations of major ions and clearer water (but no change in dissolved organic carbon) were noted in the thermokarst lakes. Significant correlations were made between the percentage of the basin affected by thermokarst and lake ionic load. In unaltered lakes, water ionic strength was most affected by fire-induced active-layer deepening. The type of surface deposits was determined to have the greatest control on lake dissolved organic carbon (DOC), with the highest DOC concentrations and color in undisturbed lakes with lacustrine catchments. Environmental factors, including surficial geology and nearness to tree line or coast, were subordinate to the main driver of water-quality variation, which was permafrost degradation.

78. **Kozlenko, N., and Jeffries, M.O., 2000, Bathymetric mapping of shallow water in thaw lakes on the North Slope of Alaska with spaceborne imaging radar: Arctic, v. 53, no. 3, p. 306–316.**
This paper demonstrates methodology that can be used to create bathymetric maps of shallow lakes on the North Slope of Alaska using spaceborne synthetic aperture radar (SAR) imaging. This technique only works for lakes or depths within lakes that are shallower than the maximum growth of winter ice in a given year. A time series of SAR imagery was analyzed to define lake-bottom contours that transitioned from floating-ice to grounded-ice conditions during the winter, and was compared to an ice-growth model. The techniques only resulted in modest agreement between the bathymetry maps created with the SAR technique and the standard bathymetric maps acquired by sonar during the summer.

79. **Lacelle, D., Bjornson, J., and Lauriol, B., 2009, Climatic and geomorphic factors affecting contemporary (1950–2004) activity of retrogressive thaw slumps on the Aklavik Plateau, Richardson Mountains, NWT, Canada: Permafrost and Periglacial Processes, v. 21, no. 1, p. 1–15.**
This paper uses aerial photography to identify retrogressive thaw slumps on the Aklavik Plateau, in the Northwest Territories. The steps in the initiation and the morphology of the features are discussed, and the initiation and presence are compared to climate factors. Thaw

slumps in this area consist of a near-vertical headwall, a low-gradient (2–10-degree) floor, and a steeply-sloping (15–25-degree) evacuation channel that connects the slump to the river. These features are believed to have begun forming during the Holocene, and deeply buried woody material in recent slumps suggests the presence of previous slumping in the same locations, indicating a polycyclic process. The rate of thaw slump initiation doubled between the periods of 1954–1971 and 1985–2004, coinciding with increases in 10-year running mean summer air temperatures. Active mature thaw slumps decreased over the period or record, potentially related to decreasing precipitation trends.

80. **Lantuit, H., Overduin, P.P., Couture, N., Wetterich, S., Aré, F., Atkinson, D., Vasiliev, A., 2012, The Arctic Coastal Dynamics database—new classification scheme and statistics on Arctic permafrost coastlines: Estuaries and Coasts, v. 35, no. 2, p. 383–400.**
This paper presents a geomorphological classification scheme for Arctic permafrost coastlines, with information on offshore, frontshore, backshore, and onshore units. Associated with each cross-shore unit and coastal segment are attributes that describe the geomorphology, cryolithology, geochemistry, and erosion rate. The average erosion rate for the entire arctic coast was 0.5 m/yr, but locally, erosion may be greater than long-term averages of 8 m/yr. The relation between ground-ice content and erosion rate are shown in figure 7a of the paper.

81. **Lantuit, H., and Pollard, W.H., 2008, Fifty years of coastal erosion and retrogressive thaw slump activity on Herschel Island, southern Beaufort Sea, Yukon Territory, Canada: Geomorphology, p. 95, no. 1, 84–102.**
This paper presents results from a remotely sensed study on the long-term patterns of coastal erosion and retrogressive thaw slump dynamics for Herschel Island. Orthorectified air photographs from 1952 and 1970 and an Ikonos satellite image from 2000 were used. Mean coastal retreat rates for the were 0.61 m/yr for the first time period (1952-1970) and 0.45 m/yr for the second time period (1970-2000). The number and total area of retrogressive thaw slumps increased by 125 and 160 percent, respectively, during the study period (1952-2000).

82. **Lantuit, H., Pollard, W.H., Couture, N., Fritz, M., Schirrmeister, L., Meyer, H., and Hubberten, H.W., 2012, Modern and late Holocene retrogressive thaw slump activity on the Yukon Coastal Plain and Herschel Island, Yukon Territory, Canada: Permafrost and Periglacial Processes, v. 23, no. 1, p. 39–51.**
This paper quantifies environmental, sedimentological, and geochemical data from undisturbed sites and those with active and stable retrogressive thaw slumps, and found differences in slope, sedimentology, and biogeochemistry between undisturbed and slumped areas. Total organic carbon (TOC) and soil moisture were lower in slumped material. Radiocarbon ages indicated high rates of slumping 300 years ago and in the modern era, which is provided as evidence of the polycyclic nature of retrogressive thaw slumping.

83. **Lantz, T.C., and Kokelj, S.V., 2008, Increasing rates of retrogressive thaw slump activity in the Mackenzie Delta region, NWT, Canada: Geophysical Research Letters, v. 35, no. 6, L06502.**
The authors analyzed historical temperature records and mapped retrogressive thaw slumps in the Mackenzie Delta region using aerial photographs taken in 1950, 1973, and 2004. Retrogressive thaw slumps occur when ice-rich permafrost on sloping terrain thaws, exposing ice-rich soils that also thaw, and the resulting mud slurry falls to the base of the exposure. Headwalls can retreat farther during warm temperatures. Thaw slumps are common along coastlines and lakeshores in the western Arctic, and mapped slumps affected

about 8 percent of the 2,880 lakes greater than 1 ha in area examined in this study. Thaw-slump growth is related to the ice content of the thawing terrain, slump aspect, and morphology. Thaw slump rates were 1.4 times greater from 1973 to 2004 than from 1950 to 1973, suggesting that warming temperatures are influencing thaw-slump activity and can be expected to increase with continued climate change. The study did not account for disturbed terrain lost to lake expansion, which occurred in about 10 percent of studied cases. Therefore, reported growth rates are likely conservative and are lower than other rates published in the literature.

84. **Lewkowicz, A.G., 1987, Headwall retreat of ground-ice slumps, Banks Island, Northwest Territories: Canadian Journal of Earth Sciences, v. 24, no. 6, p. 1077–1085.**
This paper develops an analytical model of headwall retreat based on measured energy fluxes, temperature, wind speed, and the ice face and ground slope. Calculated rates of retreat were close to maximum rates estimated from 10 years of aerial photographs. The model compared favorably to measured rates of daily and cumulative headwall retreat, although there was significant variability. Orientation of the slump was determined to be an unimportant variable, likely because direct-beam radiation only was a part of the total input. July was considered the most important month for ice ablation; however, the ice retreat rates were 1.5–2.5 times greater than the ablation rates, depending on slump geometry. Meteorological measurements were used to accurately calculate ablation rates in circumstances where the ice is freely exposed to the inputs.

85. **Lewkowicz, A.G., 2007, Dynamics of active-layer detachment failures, Fosheim Peninsula, Ellesmere Island, Nunavut, Canada: Permafrost and Periglacial Processes, v. 18, no. 1, p. 89–103.**
This paper catalogues and analyzes several fresh active-layer detachment slides that occurred on the Fosheim Peninsula during a warm period in late summer, 2005. Some failures moved instantaneously, while others moved downslope over several days. Constraining the bright sun-air temperature relationship developed in their 2005 publication, the authors determined that 7 days of warm and bright conditions were the necessary threshold to cause a failure. This failure continued to move even as temperatures and insolation decreased. Effective stress analysis was used to explain two failures on slopes of 10–18 degrees, which were able to continue traversing low-angled terrain only given dynamic loading and very low undrained basal shear strengths.

86. **Lewkowicz, A.G., and Harris, C., 2005, Frequency and magnitude of active-layer detachment failures in discontinuous and continuous permafrost, northern Canada: Permafrost and Periglacial Processes, v. 16, no. 1, p. 115–130.**
This study compares active layer detachment failures that occurred weeks to months after a fire in the discontinuous permafrost zone, and those failures generated rapidly by summer conditions in the continuous permafrost zone. The importance of threshold meteorological conditions and pre-conditioning of the active layer was noted. Post-fire slides occurred after the permafrost thawed, whereas, in the continuous permafrost zones, failures were related to the rapid thawing of ice lenses in the bottom of the active layer. Failures were more dependent on ground ice and surficial deposits than insolation, and failures were more prevalent on the north-facing slopes in the discontinuous permafrost zone where thermal disturbance was largest. Fire led to rapid geomorphic work, but over the longer term, warming of slopes in the continuous permafrost zone led to the greatest geomorphic work. The authors observed a surface heating threshold dependent on bright sunshine and daily air

temperatures that, if maintained for 9–13 days, could lead to failures on the Fosheim Peninsula.

87. **Lewkowicz, A.G., and Harris, C., 2005, Morphology and geotechnique of active-layer detachment failures in discontinuous and continuous permafrost, northern Canada: Geomorphology, v. 69, no. 1, p. 275–297.**

This study compares 50 active-layer detachment failures caused by fire to several hundred such failures caused by summer meteorological triggers. Morphology and morphometry were similar for sites in the different permafrost zones, and mesoscale geomorphic factors also significantly control morphometry. Failures were categorized by morphology, and two main types were observed: (1)compact forms, which are bell-shaped and relatively small (less than 30 m) with little internal deformation; and (2) elongated forms, which are trapezoidal or hourglass-shaped, tens of meters long, with severely deformed toe slope sediments indicating higher velocities and greater inertia. Slope-stability tests indicated that failures in the discontinuous permafrost zone resulted from high pore pressures during rapid thawing of ice-rich permafrost. In the continuous permafrost zone, failures require pre-conditioning of the basal shear zone by annual solifluction or ice-lens development, which reduces shear strengths such that a periodic extreme event may trigger the slide.

88. **Lewis, K.C., Zyvoloski, G.A., Travis, B., Wilson, C., and Rowland, J., 2012, Drainage subsidence associated with Arctic permafrost degradation: Journal of Geophysical Research—Earth Surface (2003–2012), v. 117, no. F4.**

This paper creates a model capable of handling water and heat transport, freeze thaw, and ground subsidence. An analytical solution of a thawing soil column initially is derived, and the output is compared to the Finite Element Heat and Mass Transfer model (FEHM). These analytical solutions may be applicable to situations with variable permeabilities if an appropriate average permeability is chosen. The FEHM then is combined with a freeze-thaw model, which is tested using the common frozen wall benchmark problem. The rates of simulated subsidence compared well to actual conditions. The model did not use a time-varying upper boundary condition, and, therefore, could be different given actual conditions in the Arctic. However, given that drainage and slumping can occur on weekly time scales, the true control may be a matter of initial thaw and drainage initiation.

89. **Liljedahl, A.K., Hinzman, L.D., and Schulla, J., 2012, Ice-wedge polygon type controls low-gradient watershed-scale hydrology, *in* Hinkel, K.M., ed., Tenth International Conference on Permafrost, Vol. 1—International Contributions: Salekhard, Russia, The Northern Publisher, p. 231–236.**

A coupled surface, unsaturated, and saturated zone hydrologic model was used to simulate runoff from patterned ground dominated either by low- or high-centered polygons. Catchment water storage and evapotranspiration were higher in the low-centered polygon model owing to storage of water in ponds on top of each polygon. Runoff was higher and evapotranspiration was lower in the high-centered polygon model, because of the lack of storage potential in the high-centered polygons, and drainage to and export from the trough network. Because permafrost thaw may lead to polygons transitioning from low- to high-centered polygons, warming may result in decreased water storage and evapotranspiration potential from Arctic soils. However, , this model used a homogeneous domain, whereas, in reality, landscapes contain both low- and high-centered polygons as well as trough and other thermokarst ponds, which may buffer these hydrologic shifts.

90. **Lin, Z., Niu, F., Xu, Z., Xu, J., and Wang, P., 2010, Thermal regime of a thermokarst lake and its influence on permafrost, Beiluhe Basin, Qinghai-Tibet Plateau. Permafrost and Periglacial Processes, p. 21, no. 4, p. 315–324.**
This paper examined the spatial distribution of permafrost under and around a thermokarst lake, and monitored lakeshore retrogression. Eighty percent of the shoreline collapsed each year, with most of the collapse occurring in the late summer. Thaw depths were greater on the lakeshore relative to the surrounding terrain, and there appeared to be a through-going talik in the lake bottom. The lake bottom temperature ranged from 2 to 10°C, and the warm lake created a large thaw bulb and thermal signature that could be detected in the sub-permafrost ground many tens of meters from the lake edge.

91. **Ling, F., and Zhang, T., 2004, Modeling study of talik freeze-up and permafrost response under drained thaw lakes on the Alaskan Arctic Coastal Plain: Journal of Geophysical Research, v. 109, no. D1, D01111.**
This paper presents a heat transport model to calculate the time needed for the talik beneath a lake to refreeze following lake drainage. Three initial ground temperature conditions were considered, and taliks of 28, 43, and 53 m thickness were determined to refreeze in 40, 106, and 157 years, respectively. Refreezing is slowed significantly by the latent heat of fusion needed to change water from a liquid to solid form. The authors recognized that a model also capable of handling advective heat transport owing to the flow of water in the talik would result in a more accurate result.

92. **Ling, F., Wu, Q., Zhang, T., and Niu, F., 2012, Modelling open talik formation and permafrost lateral thaw under a thermokarst lake, Beiluhe Basin, Qinghai Tibet Plateau: Permafrost and Periglacial Processes, v. 23, no. 4, p. 312–321.**
This paper uses a two-dimensional unsteady finite-element model with heat transfer and phase change to model talik formation in a study lake. Thermokarst lakes constitute a major heat source capable of raising ground temperatures in the surrounding terrain, and the greatest mean thaw rate (24.8 cm/y) occurred within the first 50 years after lake formation,

93. **Little, J.D., Sandall, H., Walegur, M.T., and Nelson, F.E., 2003, Application of differential global positioning systems to monitor frost heave and thaw settlement in tundra environments: Permafrost and Periglacial Processes, v. 14, no. 4, p. 349–357.**
This paper describes the use of differential Global Positioning Systems (DGPS) for monitoring seasonal and annual frost heave and thaw settlement on the Arctic Coastal Plain of northern Alaska. The authors developed acrylite (durable lightweight plastic), tube-shaped platform targets with a prong-like bottom. The targets were about 20 cm long and 2.5 cm in diameter. The targets were installed towards the end of the thaw season. The time required to make measurements at the targets varied from less than 1minute for stop-and-go kinematic to more than 10 minutes for rapid static DGPS survey mode. Using the rapid static configuration, the authors surveyed a field site composed of 30 targets using the rapid static survey method in 5–8 hours with a vertical error of about 1.5 cm. When these surveys were repeated within and among years, the authors measured about 1–2 cm of heave associated with the freeze-up period and 4–5 cm of subsidence at the time of maximum summer thaw. The advantages of DGPS include great accuracy and automatic placement of surveys within well-established geodetic coordinate systems. Drawbacks involve high costs, target reinsertion difficulties, and physical demands. DGPS entails significant time requirements compared to traditional leveling techniques when surveying small areas. However, DGPS has the potential to measure large regions much more rapidly than classical methods.

94. **Liu, L., Zhang, T., and Wahr, J., 2010, InSAR measurements of surface deformation over permafrost on the North Slope of Alaska: Journal of Geophysical Research, v. 115, no. F3, F03023.**
This paper describes the use of interferometric synthetic aperture radar (InSAR) for the measurement of vertical surface deformation (heave and thaw) for a 50-by-100-km region on the North Slope of Alaska centered on Prudhoe Bay and the Sag River. ERS-1 and ERS-2 satellite imagery was used. Seasonal vertical movement of typical tundra settings was about 1–4 cm. However, between 1992 and 2000, the land surface moved downward at a rate of 1–4 cm per decade, which was interpreted as thawing of ice-rich permafrost in the transient layer or near the permafrost table. Lowering of ground surface as a result of increased thaw could partially explain the absence of a trend in active layer thickness increases over the same time period.

95. **Liu, L., Schaefer, K., Zhang, T., and Wahr, J., 2012, Estimating 1992–2000 average active layer thickness on the Alaskan North Slope from remotely sensed surface subsidence: Journal of Geophysical Research, v. 117, no. F1, F01005.**
This paper shows the usefulness of measuring active-layer thickness from thaw-season surface subsidence based on interferometric synthetic aperture radar (InSAR). An algorithm was developed that accounts for the vertical distribution of water content in the active layer, factoring in soil texture, organic matter, and moisture content, which can be used to estimate active-layer thickness based on the measurements of vertical surface deformation from the InSAR data. This algorithm was applied to ERS-1 and ERS-2 satellite InSAR-derived measurements for an 80-by-100-km area centered on Prudhoe Bay, Alaska, between 1992 and 2000 to determine average active-layer thickness at relatively high resolution. Active-layer thickness values were reported to be within 10–20 cm of what was interpreted as reality and were based on the Circumpolar Active Layer Monitoring (CALM) program grids in the region. The estimated active layer thickness was 30–50 cm in moist tundra areas and 50–80 cm in wet tundra areas. This method could complement ground-based measurements and could be useful for closing the spatial gaps of in-place measurements in remote permafrost areas and for advancing our understanding of changes in the active layer and permafrost system.

96. **Lloyd, A.H., Yoshikawa, K., Fastie, C.L., Hinzman, L., and Fraver, M., 2003, Effects of permafrost degradation on woody vegetation at arctic treeline on the Seward Peninsula, Alaska: Permafrost and Periglacial Processes, v. 14, no. 2, p. 93–101.**
This paper examined how climate-induced changes in active-layer thickness and soil drainage influences advancement of the treeline on the Seward Peninsula, Alaska. The authors measured active-layer thickness, soil moisture, density of tall shrub species, and cover of low shrub species, and reconstructed white spruce establishment history along transects across the banks of a network of thaw ponds. Transects covered topographical types, including channels (low-lying depressions at the elevation of the thaw ponds), banks (the scarp at the edge of the thaw ponds and low-lying depressions), and flats (the level terrain at the top of the banks), and included sites with and without trees and shrubs. The authors counted and tagged each tree, measured tree characteristics, and took core samples to examine growth patterns; counted density of tall shrub stems; and counted other shrub species as a visual estimate of percent cover. Active-layer depth was measured in late August using a thaw-depth probe. Soil moisture was measured as volumetric soil water content using a dielectric constant measuring device inserted in the soil. Active-layer thickness did not vary along transects, but soils on thaw-pond banks were much drier than those on level tundra or thaw-pond channels. Furthermore, thaw-pond banks were the only

sites where were successfully established, and shrubs were taller and more dominated by tall shrub species (for example, willow and shrub birch) than in other areas. The authors speculated that tree and shrub advancement in the tundra depends on well-drained microsites, such as microsites on thaw-pond banks, and, therefore, that treeline advancement is contingent on further degradation of existing permafrost.

97. **Lougheed, V.L., Butler, M.G., McEwen, D.C., and Hobbie, J.E., 2011, Changes in tundra pond limnology—Re-sampling Alaskan ponds after 40 years: Ambio, v. 40, no. 6, p. 589–599.**
This paper documents the resampling of several ponds near Barrow, Alaska, that were studied intensively in the 1970s, and found that the ponds had undergone a change in their physical, chemical, and biological characteristics. Differences included higher daily mean and maximum pond temperatures, higher concentrations of ammonia, nitrate, and soluble reactive phosphorus, and a marginal increase in phytoplankton biomass. The authors noted that it is difficult to make any broad statements regarding the effects of climate on these ponds given the small amount of data, and suggested that these ponds represent a unique and valuable long-term dataset and should be sampled more frequently and maintained as Barrow expands.

98. **MacLean, R., Oswood, M.W., Irons, J.G., and McDowell, W.H., 1999, The effect of permafrost on stream biogeochemistry—A case study of two streams in the Alaskan (USA) taiga: Biogeochemistry, v. 47, no. 3, p. 239–267.**
This paper examines the effect of permafrost on stream chemistry by analyzing soils chemistry in shallow organic soils and groundwater derived from springs and wells. Extensive permafrost led to a greater hydrograph response to spring thaw and summer storms, as well as a stronger signature of organic soil chemistry in the stream. Nitrogen cycling appeared to occur independent of permafrost extent, as indicated by limited correlations between nitrogen and discharge. A conceptual model is provided, indicating different flowpaths through organic and mineral soils, depending on permafrost extent.

99. **Mackay, J.R., 1970, Disturbances to the tundra and forest tundra environment of the western Arctic: Canadian Geotechnical Journal, v. 7, no. 4, p. 420–432.**
The e terms thermokarst and thermo-erosion are defined, and differences between these two terms are highlighted, particularly the importance of thermal degradation and vertical subsidence of thermokarst versus the importance of thermal degradation, mechanical erosion, and lateral expansion under the influence of flowing water for thermo-erosion. The author uses multiple examples from Northern Canada to explain his views of these processes. Examples include the impact of man-made disturbances from seismic exploration, a wildfire, a seepage in a channel, and a dog kennel patch on underlying permafrost. Field-measured rates of thermokarst and thermo-erosion are reported for each of these examples.

100. **Mackay, J.R., 1972, The world of underground ice: Annals of the Association of American Geographers, v. 62, no. 1, p. 1–22.**
This paper provides an overview of the types and forms of ground ice. The paper includes a map of permafrost distribution across the northern hemisphere, and a schematic indicating how different processes lead to different forms of ground ice. The paper discusses many forms of ground ice and how they originate and thaw, and describes the formation of three pingos on the coastal plain at length. The potential for ice to exist beneath the ocean is also noted.

101. **Mackay, J.R., 1998, Pingo growth and collapse, Tuktoyaktuk Peninsula area, western Arctic coast, Canada—A long-term field study: Géographie physique et Quaternaire, v. 52, no. 3, p. 271–323.**
This paper presents results from repeat topographical surveys on 11pingos in the western Canadian Arctic over a 20–25 year period. The paper focuses on pingo genesis; the role of pore water expulsion when saturated sands freeze; long-term pingo growth data; sub-pingo water lenses; hydrofracturing, peripheral faulting, and spring flow; and pingo collapse. One pingo in the study area grew by 4.5 m during the study period. Information is presented on two pulsating pingos that showed signs of increased and decreased height during the study period. Several mechanisms responsible for pingo collapse also are discussed.

102. **Mackay, J.R., and Burn, C.R., 2002, The first 20 years (1978–1979 to 1998–1999) of active-layer development, Illisarvik experimental drained lake site, western Arctic coast, Canada: Canadian Journal of Earth Sciences, v. 39, no. 11, p. 1657–1674.**
This paper presents information on active-layer thickness, snow depth, soil temperature, near-surface ground ice, soil heave, and permafrost temperature in the 20 years following the artificial drainage of a lake in the western Canadian Arctic. Permafrost began to aggrade the year following the lake drainage. However, as vegetation colonized the basin floor, snow accumulation increased as well as the active layer. The rate of growth of aggradational ice in the permafrost has been 0.5 cm/yr over the first 20 years since the lake drainage was induced.

103. **Mackay, J.R., and Burn, C.R., 2002, The first 20 years (1978–1979 to 1998–1999) of ice-wedge growth at the Illisarvik experimental drained lake site, western Arctic coast, Canada: Canadian Journal of Earth Sciences, v. 39, no. 1, p. 95–111.**
This paper provides information on the growth of ice wedges in a drained lake basin over a 20-year period following the artificial drainage of the lake in the western Canadian Arctic. Ice wedges began to grow the year immediately following drainage but had stopped growing any further 12 years post-drainage. This was a result of vegetation growth in the basin and associated snow accumulation in the basin.

104. **Maher, A.I., Treitz, P.M., and Ferguson, M.A., 2012, Can Landsat data detect variations in snow cover within habitats of arctic ungulates?: Wildlife Biology, v. 18, no. 1, p. 75–87.**
Modeling suggests increased snow cover in the warming Arctic may affect ungulate populations through reduced food access in winter. This paper examined whether satellite imagery could be used to predict snow cover and snow depth at the landscape level to better predict ungulate population dynamics. Landsat imagery was used to estimate field-measured percent snow-covered area (F-SCA) and to develop a threshold for a normalized difference snow index (NDSI) in wintering areas of the Peary caribou herd in the Bathurst Islands, Northwest Territories, Canada. An NDSI threshold of 0.7 instead of 0.4 used in previous literature was more correlated to total snowfall or snow depth than using the nearest weather station, and could detect winters with relatively mild snow-cover conditions, but not those with very severe conditions. The authors recommended development of greater NDSI thresholds and suggested that these methods might be more useful for southern Arctic regions where sun angles would be less limiting than in the Bathurst Islands.

105. **Marsh, P., Russell, M., Pohl, S., Haywood, H., and Onclin, C., 2008, Changes in thaw lake drainage in the Western Canadian Arctic from 1950 to 2000: Hydrological Processes, v. 23, no. 1, p. 145–158.**

This paper assesses the drainage of thermokarst lakes between 1950 and 2000 for a 10,000-km^2 study area in the western Canadian Arctic on the east side of the MacKenzie Delta. The authors used a combination of historical aerial photographs and topographic maps to determine lake drainage events in three time periods: 1950–1973, 1973–1985, and 1985–2000. Between 1950 and 2000, 41 lakes drained in the study region for a rate of 0.82 lakes per year; however, when drainage events are assessed per time period, the lake drainage rate has decreased from 1.13 to 0.83 to 0.30 lakes per year, respectively. The minimum lake mapping unit in this study was unclear, as were the factors responsible for the reduction in the number of lake drainage events across time. Based on modeling and hydrological observations, one lake that drained in 1989 was believed to result from a combination of a warm summer, a resulting deep active layer, and a moderately high lake level.

106. **Matell, N., Anderson, R.S., Overeem, I., Wobus, C., Urban, F.E., and Clow, G.D., 2013, Modeling the subsurface thermal impact of Arctic thaw lakes in a warming climate; Computers and Geosciences, v. 53, p. 69–79.**

This paper uses a one-dimensional model combining heat conduction, lake ice, and subsidence to evaluate temperature as a function of depth in thermokarst lakes. Modeled scenarios involved simulating talik formation in lakes with different depths. A lake depth threshold was recognized, such that lakes deeper than about 1.25 m are capable of significantly altering the thermal state of the subsurface, resulting in talik formation and subsidence.

107. **McRoberts, E.C., and Morgenstern, N.R., 1974, The stability of thawing slopes: Canadian Geotechnical Journal, v. 11, no. 4, p. 447–469.**

This study provides a review of the common types of thaw-dominated landslides. A common force balance used in the geotechnical field, the factor of safety, is used to show that slides should not be occurring on the low-angled slopes on which they are observed, unless thaw-consolidation can provide additional water to increase pore pressures. Two mass movement models, the thaw-consolidation model and the ablation model, are considered. The importance of removing vegetation to begin the thaw process is recognized.

108. **Mesquita, P.S., Wrona, F.J., and Prowse, T.D., 2010, Effects of retrogressive permafrost thaw slumping on sediment chemistry and submerged macrophytes in Arctic tundra lakes: Freshwater Biology, v. 55, no. 11, p. 2347–2358.**

This study compares lake water chemistry, sediment chemistry, and physical parameters, as well as macrophyte biomass and community structure from three undisturbed lakes and five lakes with retrogressive thaw slumps. There was no difference in water-column nutrients for the disturbed lakes compared to the undisturbed lakes, but the disturbed lakes had higher electrical conductivity and pH. Disturbed lake sediments had lower organic matter concentrations and higher concentrations of many macro and micro nutrients. Disturbed lakes had higher transparency and macrophyte biomass, and were dominated by mosses. Light attenuation was the only significant variable that explained macrophyte distribution patterns.

109. **Michel, F.A., and Van Everdingen, R.O., 1994, Changes in hydrogeologic regimes in permafrost regions due to climatic change: Permafrost and Periglacial Processes, v. 5, no. 3, 191–195.**
This paper summarizes the effects of climate change on groundwater systems in permafrost regions. Subsurface aquifers have the potential to develop as permafrost thaws, and this may have substantial implications for regional groundwater flow, as well as for river discharge and chemistry.

110. **Morgenstern, A., Grosse, G., Guenther, F., Fedorova, I., and Schirrmeister, L., 2011, Spatial analyses of thermokarst lakes and basins in yedoma landscapes of the Lena Delta: The Cryosphere, v. 5, p. 849–867.**
This paper presents a GIS analysis of thermokarst lakes and basins on three different aged land surfaces on the Lena Delta in Siberia. Lakes were manually extracted from a Landsat-7 ETM+ satellite image and basins were manually mapped at a scale of 1:30,000. Lakes covered only 5 percent of the study region. Adding the presence of drained basins to the assessment of the effect of thermokarst on the landscape increased the estimate to 22 percent. These findings are placed in the context of the potential for future areas of the study region to experience thermokarst development.

111. **Murdoch, A., and Power, M., 2013, The effect of lake morphometry on thermal habitat use and growth in Arctic char populations—Implications for understanding climate-change impacts: Ecology of Freshwater Fish, v. 22, no. 3, p. 453–466 (published online first).**
This paper reconstructs historical temperatures from Arctic charr otoliths sampled from small, shallow and large, deeper thermokarst lakes in Ungava Bay, Quebec, Canada. Oxygen stable isotope temperature reconstruction methods were used to estimate temperatures. Water temperature averaged 13.1°C and growth rates ranged from about 50 to 85 mm/year. There was weak evidence that growth of the fish in the smaller lake increased with age through increased use of cooler thermal habitats, but no such relationship was observed in the larger lake. However, increasing air temperatures significantly decreased growth rates in the smaller and shallower lake, possibly because of warmer surface and littoral waters and limited preferred cool-water habitat. This relationship was not found in the larger and deeper lake. The authors suggested that char were not as vulnerable to the impacts of temperature warming in the larger lake, possibly because of better behavioral thermoregulation opportunities in a cooler, deeper lake.

112. **Murton, J.B., 2001, Thermokarst sediments and sedimentary structures, Tuktoyaktuk coastlands, western Arctic Canada: Global and Planetary Change, v. 28, no. 1, p. 175–192.**
This study provides evidence of substantial thermokarsting activity associated with a warm period on the Arctic Coast between 10 and 9 thousand years (ka) Before Present (BP). Many types of themokarsts are categorized, and the most distinctive types are suggested as follows: 1) peaty diamicton deposited mainly by debris flows in retrogressive thaw slumps, 2) a basal unit of diamicton in thermokarst-basin sequences attributed to progradation of material transported into thaw lakes by thaw slumping around their margins, 3) involutions attributed to soft-sediment deformation during active-layer deepening; and 4) casts of ice and composite wedges. The authors assert that these forms are caused by the thaw of excessive ice, and suggest that some of these structures may have been or could be mistakenly classified as glacial deposits in other studies.

113. **Murton, J.B., 2013, Ground ice and cryostratigraphy *in* Shroder, J., and others, eds., Treatise on geomorphology: San Diego, Academic Press, v. 8, Glacial and Periglacial Geomorphology, p. 173–201.**

This book chapter provides a review on ground ice and cryostratigraphy—the stratigraphic analysis of ice-rich permafrost. The description and genesis of ice in frozen ground are reviewed and demonstrated through case studies related to 1) the transition zone at the top of permafrost, (2) massive ice and icy sediments, (3) ice wedges, and (4) yedoma and related deposits. A section is also included on mapping ground ice. Detailed information on cryostructures in permafrost is given in table 1 of the chapter, and information on cryofacies of frozen sediments is given in table 2. The chapter concludes with a recommendation on future research needs in the field of crystratigraphy.

114. **Nelson, F.E., Hinkel, K.M., Shiklomanov, N.I., Mueller, G.R., Miller, L.L., and Walker, D.A., 1998, Active-layer thickness in north central Alaska—Systematic sampling, scale, and spatial autocorrelation: Journal of Geophysical Research, v. 103, no. D22, p. 28963–28973.**

This paper measures active-layer depth at many sites with a wide range of terrain, soil, and vegetation characteristics across the Arctic Coastal Plain and Arctic Foothills, Alaska. Along 100-m grids at 7 sites, a graduated steel rod was placed in the soil to measure active-layer depth. The authors evaluated their approach and found that the depth at probe resistance corresponds closely to the frost table. They observed high spatial, but low temporal heterogeneity in active-layer depth that varied between the coastal plain and the foothills. Samples were taken during 2 years with similar air temperatures, which may explain the low temporal variability in active-layer depth. Active-layer thickness was influenced by microclimate, hydrology, soil moisture, and vegetation. This authors attempted to use a network of monitoring sites that were established to collect a wide range of ecological data across northern Alaska. The authors learned, however, that, although the 100-m scale was suitable for the coastal plain, narrow water tracks and tussock tundra in the foothills led to variations in thaw depth over short lateral distances. Reconnaissance sampling in this area was recommended to determine the appropriate sampling scale for particular variables.

115. **Nicol, S., Roach, J.K., and Griffith, B., Spatial heterogeneity in statistical power to detect changes in lake area in Alaskan National Wildlife Refuges: Landscape Ecology, p. 1–11.**

This paper investigates how the statistical power to detect trends in lake sizes in the National Wildlife Refuges of Alaska are affected by the area of analysis and the number of years of monitoring. The authors used large study areas (930–4,560 km^2) and smaller cells (2.6–25.9 km^2) during 4–50-year periods, and observed that trends could be detected within 5–15 years, that trends smaller than 2.0percent per year required more than 50 years to detect, and that there was substantial spatial variation in the time required to detect changes among the smaller cells. The authors suggested that even small trends may be ecologically meaningful, and so long-term monitoring should be established as early as possible.

116. **Niu, F., Lin, Z., Liu, H., and Lu, J., 2011, Characteristics of thermokarst lakes and their influence on permafrost in Qinghai-Tibet Plateau: Geomorphology, v. 132, no. 3, p. 222–233.**

This study focused on regional-scale characteristics of the lakes near the Qinghai-Tibet Railroad, with narrower foci on the chemistry of 11 lakes and permafrost configuration in 1 lake. Lake depth was observed to vary from 0.4–3 m, with most lakes freezing to the bottom during the winter. More lakes were present in the ice-rich permafrost regions, and lake salinity varied greatly, from 0.36 to 30.17 g/L across regions. The intensively studied lake was determined to be 890 years old based on cesium-137 and lead-210 isotope dating. No ice was observed beneath the center of the intensively studied lake (to 60 m), which was attributed to an open talik.

117. **Osterkamp, T.E., and Jorgenson, M.T., 2009, Permafrost conditions and processes, *in* Young, Rob, and Norby, Lisa, eds., Geological Monitoring: Boulder, Colorado, Geological Society of America, p. 205–227.**

This paper provides a perspective on permafrost stability, the cause for concern given current and predicted climate trends, and the need for establishing a monitoring network to better understand the patterns and processes of thermokarst development to plan for potential effects and for developing reasonable responses to them. Recommendations are made for developing standard methods for thermokarst monitoring that focus on changes that have already occurred, current state of the landscape, and monitoring of potential future change. Monitoring should start with proper site selection that is best guided by a map, model, or general understanding of permafrost distribution and characteristics in a given area. Other factors to consider when developing a long-term monitoring site include access, availability of long-term climate data, terrain, snow cover, hydrology, geology, vegetation, and security. A series of steps related to monitoring the vital signs (thermal and physical conditions) of permafrost stability also is provided. For monitoring the permafrost thermal state (from simple to more complex), the following steps (or levels) apply: Level 1 includes the determination of a frozen or thawed state through probing, Level 2 incorporates permafrost surface temperature monitoring with data loggers, and Level 3 incorporates deep, vertical permafrost temperature borehole logging. For monitoring physical conditions, the following steps (or levels) apply: Level 1 includes mapping the presence, absence, or both, of thermokarst features from field or aerial observations or sampling strategies, Level 2 involves the establishment of photographic trend plots and topographic surveys related to thaw settlement, and Level 3 involves soil and ground ice stratigraphy sampling and description and incorporation of remote sensing for inventorying and change detection analysis. The authors provided three key questions that one should ask during the study design phase: (1) Is permafrost present, and is there any evidence that is has thawed in the past?, (2) What is the current thermal state of the permafrost, and what is the current extent of the thawing?, and (3) What is the projected future thermal state of the permafrost, and what are the rates and characteristics of change associated with thermokarst terrain? The paper concludes with a case study and rough cost estimates for developing a comprehensive permafrost condition and thermokarst monitoring program.

118. **Osterkamp, T.E., and Romanovsky, V.E., 1996, Characteristics of changing permafrost temperatures in the Alaskan Arctic, USA: Arctic and Alpine Research, v. 28, no. 3, p. 267-273.**

The paper presents results on permafrost temperature readings in northern Alaska from 1983 to 1993 at both deep borehole and shallow ground temperature monitoring sites. Simulations r also are made between the 1-m-deep and 20-m-deep readings to complete data gaps associated with lack of monitoring equipment at intermediate depths. The data show that the permafrost in northern Alaska began to warm at the end of the 1980s.

119. **Parsekian, A.D., Grosse, G., Walbrecker, J.O., Müller-Petke, M., Keating, K., Liu, L., and Knight, R., 2013, Detecting unfrozen sediments below thermokarst lakes with surface nuclear magnetic resonance: Geophysical Research Letters, v. 40, no. 3, p. 535–540.**

The authors use a geophysical method to determine frozen and unfrozen conditions under thermokarst lakes in the Fairbanks, Alaska, region. The method, Nuclear Magnetic Resonance, allows a point measurement of talik depth. The authors were able to image a situation with a closed-talik and an open-talik. They also were able to image the base of the permafrost in a terrestrial setting.

120. **Parsekian, A.D., Jones, B.M., Jones, M., Grosse, G., Anthony, W., Katey, M., and Slater, L., 2011, Expansion rate and geometry of floating vegetation mats on the margins of thermokarst lakes, northern Seward Peninsula, Alaska, USA: Earth Surface Processes and Landforms, v. 36, no. 14, p. 1889–1897.**

This paper describes the formation of floating vegetation mats on the margin of expanding thermokarst lakes on the northern Seward Peninsula between 1950 and 2007. These features have been described widely in boreal ecosystems in Alaska but seldom have been described in arctic tundra settings. Based on ground-penetrating radar, the vegetation mats were an estimated 60 cm thick and, based on probing and temperature measurements, the water below the vegetation mat remained thawed during the winter and a talik 4 m or more thick developed beneath the mat while the lake froze completely to its bottom. The maximum expansion rate of the floating mat feature into the adjacent tundra through permafrost degradation was 1–2 m/yr. Including the area associated with these mats increased the land area subject to permafrost degradation by 4 percent between 1950 and 2006.

121. **Peterson, K.M., and Billings, W.D., 1980, Tundra vegetational patterns and succession in relation to microtopography near Atkasook, Alaska: Arctic and Alpine Research, p. 473–482.**

This paper provides an overview on vegetation distribution and succession as it relates to microtopography that results from various geomorphic agents acting in the area near Atqasuk, Alaska. Information is given on vegetation patterns related to ice wedges, river banks and river meandering, and wind action. Two examples of the role of animals on vegetation patterns in the region also are presented.

122. **Plug, L.J., and West, J.J., 2009, Thaw lake expansion in a two-dimensional coupled model of heat transfer, thaw subsidence, and mass movement: Journal of Geophysical Research—Earth Surface (2003–2012), v. 114, no. F1.**

This paper presents a model that combines key factors controlling thermokarst lake expansion: heat transfer and thawing of lake banks, and movement of thawed materials away from the shore. The model was created to simulate two systems from the Seward Peninsula and the Yukon Coastal Plain, and the resulting lakeshore profiles were determined to be broadly consistent with actual lakes. Lakes from the Seward Peninsula expanded more rapidly, even under identical climates, which the authors attributed to their deeper basins and steeper bathymetric slopes that move thawed material away from the lake margins. An increase in mean annual air temperatures of 3°C could increase lake expansion rates by 1.5–2.5 times. The model was used to show that a temperature decrease of 8°C would halt lake expansion, which is consistent with paleo-studies indicating that the basins formed because of postglacial warming. The model shows that thaw basins expand monotonically, but the lakes do not. Therefore, measuring basin changes may be the best way to detect thermokarst acceleration related to climate.

123. **Prowse, T., Alfredsen, K., Beltaos, S., Bonsal, B.R., Bowden, W.B., Duguay, C.R., and Weyhenmeyer, G.A., 2011, Effects of changes in arctic lake and river ice: AMBIO, A Journal of the Human Environment, v. 40, p. 63–74.**
This paper summarizes the hydrological, ecological, and socio-economic consequences of climate-change-mediated changes to freshwater ice in the Arctic. Key impacts include changes to low flows, lake evaporation regimes and water levels, and the timing and severity of river-ice break-up. River geomorphology, vegetation regimes, and nutrient-sediment fluxes that sustain aquatic ecosystems are particularly sensitive to changes in the severity and timing of river-ice break-up. Both positive and negative effects of these changes on stream biota are possible. Changes in ice-induced hydrological connectivity and lake stratification could lead to the loss of some species and the establishment of others. Socio-economic factors affected include transportation and hydroelectric production. Ice roads may no longer be feasible and hydroelectric potential (that is, waterflow) may increase, but changes to ice blockages and dynamic ice flow on dam infrastructure may reduce production and increase costs. Implementation of a monitoring plan that incorporates remote sensing approaches along with in-place networks of observation sites is recommended. Advancements in methods to model landscape hydrology, water-ice-air energy exchanges, in-stream hydraulics, and ice mechanics would improve prediction of river-ice regimes. Monitoring should expand from primarily physical characteristics to include effects on lentic (that is, lake) and lotic (that is, stream and river) ecosystems.

124. **Pullman, E.R., Jorgenson, M.T., and Shur, Y., 2007, Thaw settlement in soils of the Arctic Coastal Plain, Alaska: Arctic, Antarctic, and Alpine Research, v. 39, no. 3, p. 468–476.**
This paper describes a synthesis of field surveys and thaw-strain and thaw-depth measures derived from soil cores taken between 1998 and 2003 in a study region spanning from Prudhoe Bay to west of the Colville River Delta. Thaw strain was determined for each of the 108 core samples, and mean thaw strain was calculated for each of the sampled terrain units. Potential thaw settlement was estimated as the decrease in volume a frozen soil sample undergoes when thawed for individual soil horizons and the potential change in the active-layer thickness caused by surface disturbance. Therefore, thaw settlement is a function of the original thickness of the active layer, the increase of the active layer as it adjusts to disturbance at the surface, and the thaw strain of the underlying permafrost. The study area was divided into 12 terrain units and an estimate of potential thaw settlement was provided for each unit. Mean thaw settlement associated with a thickening of the active layer to 1.1 m in sandy soils associated with active meander river channels resulted in zero thaw settlement; however, the same thickening of the active layer in very ice-rich silty soils would result in a thaw settlement of about 0.9 m. The authors also scaled up their estimates to cover the various ecotypes that represent the larger Arctic Coastal Plain region. These estimates are representative of the centers of ice-wedge polygonal terrain and do not factor in thermokarst that would result from degrading ice wedges and other massive ice bodies.

125. **Regmi, P., Grosse, G., Jones, M.C., Jones, B.M., and Anthony, K.W., 2012, Characterizing post-drainage succession in thermokarst lake basins on the Seward Peninsula, Alaska with TerraSAR-X Backscatter and Landsat-based NDVI Data: Remote Sensing, v. 4, no. 12, p. 3741–3765.**
The authors report on remote sensing methods using Terra-SAR-X satellite data and Landsat-7 ETM+ data to characterize succession in drained thermokarst lake basins of different age on the Seward Peninsula, Alaska. Succession in these basins includes a shift in vegetation from highly productive meadow-like fens to typical lowland tundra, a refreezing (permafrost aggradation) of formerly unfrozen lake sediments, a reduction of soil water saturation owing to enhanced drainage, and the development of terrestrial peat soils across the course of several centuries to millennia. A good relationship was established between the TerraSAR-X signal and basin age (time since drainage).

126. **Romanovsky, V.E., Smith, S.L., and Christiansen, H.H., 2010, Permafrost thermal state in the polar Northern Hemisphere during the international polar year 2007–2009—A synthesis: Permafrost and Periglacial Processes, v. 21, no. 2, p. 106–116.**
This paper provides an overview on the thermal state of permafrost in the Northern Hemisphere and development of a permafrost monitoring program over the latter half of the 20th century. Permafrost temperatures generally have warmed since the 1980s, and the warming has been most pronounced in the cold permafrost regions or regions within the continuous permafrost zone. As of the time of publication, there were 575 ground temperature monitoring stations in the Northern Hemisphere.

127. **Rowland, J.C., Jones, C.E., Altmann, G., Bryan, R., Crosby, B.T., Hinzman, L.D., and Geernaert, G.L., 2010, Arctic landscapes in transition—Responses to thawing permafrost: Eos, Transactions American Geophysical Union, v. 91, no. 26, p. 229.**
This paper provides an overview of the critical changes occurring in the Arctic related to thawing permafrost. The authors note significant and rapid changes in the Arctic, suggesting that this system may be particularly sensitive to even small climate perturbations. Therefore, scientists need to know more about the mechanisms and feedbacks driving current landscape processes in order to better predict future changes. The authors detail many of the effects associated with thawing permafrost including redistribution of water, altered drainage networks, river discharge, sediment and nutrient movement, and release of carbon from permafrost. They discuss several factors that limit our understanding and predictions of landscape change, including subsurface heterogeneity and limitations in quantifying ground ice, feedbacks between thaw and vegetation, and difficulty in numerical simulations of these processes. The authors suggest that a more integrated approach is needed to understand the drivers of change, the geomorphic response to these drivers, and the potential feedbacks between physical, chemical, and biological components of the Arctic system.

128. **Rowland, J.C., Travis, B.J., and Wilson, C.J., 2011, The role of advective heat transport in talik development beneath lakes and ponds in discontinuous permafrost: Geophysical Research Letters, v. 38, no. 17, p. L17504.**

This paper presents a model of sub-lake talik development in warm, discontinuous permafrost with and without advective heat transport. Advective heat transport is widely recognized as a critical component of permafrost degradation, but few studies have considered this. The model shows that stable permafrost thicknesses are 2–5 times greater in the absence of groundwater flow. Small variations in heat fluxes transmitted through a high hydraulic conductivity zone of the model had large effects on permafrost presence and talik development.

129. **Rydberg, J., Klaminder, J., Rosén, P., and Bindler, R., 2010, Climate driven release of carbon and mercury from permafrost mires increases mercury loading to sub-arctic lakes: Science of the Total Environment, v. 408, no. 20, p. 4778–4783.**

This paper uses cores in peat and lakebed sediments to address the timing of mercury buildup in the environment, and the potential for this mercury to be released as permafrost thaws. Long-term changes in climate, permafrost, and mire dynamics can greatly affect the movement of mercury from the mires to the lakes. Significant variability in mercury movement rates were noted during the pre-industrial era, with higher rates associated with a warm period from the 1400s to mid-1500s. Present-day rates also were high. Similar studies should be conducted to observe spatial variability in these processes. Given that mercury is a neurotoxin that bioaccumulates in fish and humans, such studies are increasingly important as permafrost thaws and more mercury may be released from Arctic watersheds.

130. **Saalfeld, S.T., Lanctot, R.B., Brown, S.C., Saalfeld, D.T., Johnson, J.A., Andres, B.A., and Bart, J.R., 2013, Predicting breeding shorebird distributions on the Arctic Coastal Plain of Alaska: Ecosphere, v. 4, no. 1, p. art16.**

This paper examines habitat relationships for eight species of shorebirds that commonly breed on the Arctic Coastal Plain, Alaska. Presence-only modeling approaches were used to identify suitable habitat and to map current distributions throughout the North Slope. For most species, habitat suitability increased at lower elevations (that is, near the coast and river deltas) and decreased within upland habitats. Models predicted that the most suitable habitat for most species was within the National Petroleum Reserve-Alaska, with additional suitable habitat within coastal areas of the Arctic National Wildlife Refuge west to Prudhoe Bay, Alaska.

131. **Sannel, A.B.K., and Brown, I.A., 2010, High-resolution remote sensing identification of thermokarst lake dynamics in a subarctic peat plateau complex: Canadian Journal of Remote Sensing, v. 36, no. S1, p. 26–40.**

This paper tests methods that could detect meter-scale changes in thermokarst lake extent using a time series of high-resolution imagery including aerial photographs and satellite imagery. Methods developed apply to various lake forms, locations, and data types. Traditional manual delineation of lake shorelines is subjective and time- and labor-intensive. Semi-automatic remote sensing techniques were examined, including unsupervised and supervised classification and texture and high-pass filtering of imagery. All techniques failed testing and evaluation. The best method examined included multiple persons manually digitizing shorelines (plus-or-minus 1.5 m accuracy). This technique improved when the authors added binary encoding of transects perpendicular to the shoreline (plus-or-minus 0.6 m accuracy). High-resolution panchromatic images (both aerial photographs and satellite images) can be used to detect small-scale changes in lake extent on decadal time scales. When images are old or data quality is poor, manual delineation of shorelines provides the most accurate depiction. Semi-automatic classification underestimated water area in shallow lakes with aquatic vegetation, and overestimated water area in heterogeneous, fen-rich landscapes. Lakes surrounded by fens were the most difficult feature to classify.

132. **Sannel, A.B.K., and Kuhry, P., 2011, Warming-induced destabilization of peat plateau/thermokarst lake complexes: Journal of Geophysical Research, v. 116, no. G3, G03035.**
This paper uses aerial photography and satellite imagery to assess thaw-lake expansion and infilling-drainage across a climatic and permafrost gradient. Rates of lake area change were compared to climate variables, and showed some correlation to mean annual air temperature. This study recognized a temperature threshold, beyond which these landforms rapidly destabilize. This is currently occurring in the sporadic permafrost zone (mean annual air temperature of about -3°C), and will likely occur in the discontinuous permafrost zone over the next century.

133. **Schuur, E.A., Crummer, K.G., Vogel, J.G., and Mack, M.C., 2007, Plant species composition and productivity following permafrost thaw and thermokarst in Alaskan tundra: Ecosystems, v. 10, no. 2, p. 280–292.**
This paper presents research on the direct and indirect effects of permafrost degradation on plant species composition and productivity at three sites located near Healy, Alaska. The study area provided a natural gradient that ranged from undisturbed moist tundra to tundra with ice wedge degradation and permafrost thaw. The objectives of the study were to describe the changes in plant species composition and productivity that occurred as a result of permafrost degradation and to quantify changes in soil microclimate and nutrient availability. The authors observed that the sites experiencing permafrost thaw transitioned from graminoid tundra to shrub tundra and that soil nitrogen availability increased where permafrost thawed.

134. **Sellmann, P.V., Brown, J., Lewellen, R.I., McKim, H., and Merry, C., 1975, The classification and geomorphic implications of thaw lakes on the Arctic Coastal Plain, Alaska: U.S. Army Corps of Engineers, Cold Regions Research and Engineering Laboratory, Hanover, New Hampshire, Report No. CRREL RR-3244, 28 p.**
This report provides a regional classification of lakes on the Arctic Coastal Plain of northern Alaska using Landsat Multispectral Scanner (MSS) data. The authors divided the limnological landscape by lake size, development of elongate axis, orientation of elongate axis, lake density, and topography. The authors also demonstrated the use of Landsat time series during the early summer to identify lake depth based on the timing associated with lake ice melt-out.

135. **Sharkhuu, A., Sharkhuu, N., Etzelmüller, B., Heggem, E.S.F., Nelson, F.E., Shiklomanov, N.I., and Brown, J., 2007, Permafrost monitoring in the Hovsgol mountain region, Mongolia: Journal of Geophysical Research, v. 112, no. F2, F02S06.**
This paper considers the causes and consequences of thawing permafrost in the mountains of Mongolia. Borehole temperature data are provided to indicate increasing permafrost temperatures, and there is a discussion of how variations in rates and trends may be related to the subsurface material. Various landscape features resulting from thawing permafrost also are discussed. The importance of both climate and anthropogenic factors in thawing permafrost are considered. Grazing is a major cause of permafrost thaw in this area, as shown by monitoring differences in temperature and thawing degree days in soils beneath grass, low and high shrubs, and mown plots.

136. **Shiklomanov, N.I., and Nelson, F.E., 2013, Thermokarst and civil infrastructure, *in* Shroder, J.F., and others, eds., Treatise on geomorphology, v. 8: San Diego, Academic Press, p. 354–373.**
This book chapter focuses on the physical processes that occur in the upper part of permafrost terrain, which includes the active layer, the transition layer, and the development of thermokarst. The authors conceptually outline the processes by which the genesis of associated landforms and engineering problems that may result from permafrost degradation and thermokarst development can be understood. An overview is provided on the type and quantity of near-surface ground ice and the two major groups of thaw processes: those related to erosion and those related to ground subsidence or top-down thaw of permafrost. The formation of thermokarst landforms are placed in the context of the unique engineering problems encountered in permafrost regions.

137. **Short, N., Brisco, B., Couture, N., Pollard, W., Murnaghan, K., and Budkewitsch, P., 2011, A comparison of TerraSAR-X, RADARSAT-2 and ALOS-PALSAR interferometry for monitoring permafrost environments, case study from Herschel Island, Canada: Remote Sensing of Environment, v. 115, no. 12, p. 3491–3506.**
This paper compares the ability of interferometric synthetic aperture radar (InSAR) datasets derived from TerraSAR-X (X-band radar), Radarsat-2 (C-band radar), and ALOS-PALSAR (L-band radar) for detecting ground movement at a continuous permafrost site located on Herschel Island, Canada. All sensors were capable of maintaining coherence during a particular summer; however, the ALOS-PALSAR proved to be best at maintaining coherence over multiple years. This is a result of the longer wavelength and greater penetration of vegetative cover of the L-band synthetic aperture radar (SAR), which has proven to be much better at maintaining coherence over permafrost environments. The ability to monitor vertical displacement over multiple years offers the most promise for permafrost studies. The authors also tried to target the many thaw slumps on Herschel Island. They determined that InSAR was not a suitable tool for monitoring these features owing to their size, their large and abrupt movement, radar look angles, and disintegration and collapse of slump features. Based primarily on the PASLAR interferograms, the authors noted a narrow band of displacement of 20–30 cm/yr on the northern part of Herschel Island from 2007 to 2010 that is believed to be associated with coastal erosion and slope instability. InSAR is capable of identifying broad areas of subtle subsidence in gentle relief, areas of terrain instability, possibly owing to permafrost thaw or ground-ice melt and the removal of water volume, and prior to significant slumping.

138. **Shur, Y.L., and Jorgenson, M.T,. 2007, Patterns of permafrost formation and degradation in relation to climate and ecosystems: Permafrost and Periglacial Processes, v. 18, no. 1, p. 7–19.**

This paper presents a classification system for describing the complex interaction of climate and ecological processes on permafrost formation and degradation. Five types of permafrost were distinguished: (1) climate-driven; (2) climate-driven, ecosystem-modified; (3) climate-driven, ecosystem protected; (4) ecosystem-driven; and (5) ecosystem-protected. Climate-driven permafrost forms under modern-day climatic conditions in recently exposed land surfaces and primarily occurs in the continuous permafrost zone. Climate-driven, ecosystem-modified permafrost occurs in the continuous permafrost zone when vegetation succession and organic-matter accumulation lead to development of an ice-rich layer at the top of the permafrost. Climate-driven, ecosystem-protected permafrost refers to permafrost currently located in the discontinuous permafrost that initially formed as climate-driven but its stability is now a result of overlying vegetation and organic material. If this permafrost thaws, it cannot be reestablished under current climatic conditions. Ecosystem-driven permafrost forms in the discontinuous permafrost zone in poorly drained, low-lying and north-facing landscape conditions, and under strong ecosystem influence. Finally, ecosystem-protected permafrost persists as sporadic patches in warmer climates, but cannot be reestablished after disturbance. These distinctions are important because these five permafrost types react differently to disturbance and climate change.

139. **Shur, Y.L., and Osterkamp, T.E., 2007, Thermokarst: Fairbanks, University of Alaska Fairbanks, Institute of Northern Engineering, Rep. INE06.11, 50 p.**

This comprehensive report on thermokarst details the history associated with the term, essential conditions for thermokarst development, causes of thermokarst, development of thermokarst, and a focus on thermokarst lake development and enlargement. Discussion of the essential conditions for thermokarst development distinguishes between permafrost conditions (ground ice, method of permafrost formation, structures in permafrost, distribution of ice in permafrost, thaw strain) and thermal conditions (air versus soil climate, heat balance, and so on). The causes of thermokarst development are divided into large scale (climatic) or small scale (local disturbance). The development of thermokarst usually occurs as a result of (1) thaw subsidence of the upper permafrost owing to an increase in active-layer depth after surface modification, (2) thaw subsidence of the upper permafrost owing to water accumulation on the soil surface accompanied by an increase in active layer thickness, (3) permafrost degradation with retreat of the permafrost table, and (or) (4) enlargement by thermal subsidence and thermal erosion of lakes that were originally formed by processes unrelated to thermokarst. This paper contains many equations, tables, and graphics showing the various conditions and stages of thermokarst development. The section on the enlargement of thermokarst lakes contains many references related to thermokarst lake expansion rates. Most of the report is based on the Russian-language literature in an effort to make this material and these ideas accessible to English-speaking readers.

140. **Sjöberg, Y., Hugelius, G., and Kuhry, P., 2013, Thermokarst lake morphometry and erosion features in two peat plateau areas of northeast European Russia: Permafrost and Periglacial Processes, v. 24, p. 75–81.**

This paper compares physical lake characteristics relevant to erosion, sediment type, and orientation in two lowland peat plateaus in western Russia. Shoreline steepness, cracks, and depth were greater on shorelines facing northeast and southeast, and on shorelines of larger lakes. Lakes in peat substrate showed greater variability in steepness, cracks, and water depths. The lakes showed some orientation, but not as great as has been witnessed in other thermokarst lakes, which the authors attribute to a more heterogeneous substrate and the importance of secondary erosional factors such as snowdrifts. Larger lakes showed signs of heavier erosion, but erosion also is important on smaller lakes because it affects a greater proportion of the peat plateau.

141. **Smith, M.W., and Riseborough, D.W., 1996, Permafrost monitoring and detection of climate change: Permafrost and Periglacial Processes, v. 7, no. 4, p. 301–309.**
This paper develops a climate-permafrost model to determine the factors that control temperature at the top of the permafrost. The authors show that permafrost temperature monitoring may be confounded by variations in local surface and lithologic conditions, and by the annual air temperature regime. The authors suggest that temperature monitoring should be concentrated at the permafrost table that active-layer depth is not necessarily an indicator of changes in the temperature of permafrost, and that monitoring at exposed bedrock will produce the most direct signal of climate and ground thermal regime.

142. **Smith, S.L., Romanovsky, V.E., Lewkowicz, A.G., Burn, C.R., Allard, M., Clow, G.D., and Throop, J,. 2010, Thermal state of permafrost in North America—A contribution to the International Polar Year: Permafrost and Periglacial Processes, v. 21, no. 2, p. 117–135.**
This paper presents results from 350 permafrost boreholes in North America. Permafrost has been warming since the 1970s in the western Arctic and since the 1990s in eastern Canada. The rates of ground warming are variable but tend to be greatest in the tundra regions.

143. **Stieglitz, M., Déry, S.J., Romanovsky, V.E., and Osterkamp, T.E., 2003, The role of snow cover in the warming of arctic permafrost: Geophysical Research Letters, v. 30, no. 13.**
This paper highlights the role of snow cover on the permafrost thermal regime. Through the use of modeling, the authors showed that snow cover variability can affect the temperature of permafrost as much as near-surface air temperature. Trends in permafrost temperature in northern Alaska from 1983 to 1998 can be explained primarily by variability in snow cover.

144. **Suttle, K.B., Power, M.E., Levine, J.M., and McNeely, C., 2004, How fine sediment in riverbeds impairs growth and survival of juvenile salmonids: Ecological Applications, v. 14, no. 4, p. 969–974.**
This paper experimentally increased fine sediment loading into northern California rivers and examined subsequent effects on juvenile salmonids and supporting food webs. Increased fine sediment decreased growth and survival of juvenile steelhead trout, and decreases were associated with a shift in invertebrates toward burrowing taxa unavailable as prey and increased steelhead activity and injury at higher levels of fine sediment. Growth decreased from about 0.23 mm/d in areas of no fine sediment to about 0.06 mm/d in areas with 100 percent embedded substrate. The results suggested that there is no threshold below which exacerbation of fine-sediment and storage in gravel-bedded rivers is harmless, but that any reduction in fine sediment loading could immediately benefit salmonids.

145. Swanson, D.K., 1996, Susceptibility of permafrost soils to deep thaw after forest fires in interior Alaska, USA, and some ecologic implications: Arctic and Alpine Research, p. 217–227.

This study analyzes vegetation and soil data from many burned and unburned (no fire in more than 100 years) sites in the Kobuk Preserve in interior Alaska. Burned sites were divided into three groups: frozen, thawed, or dry, depending on their pre- and post-fire state. These three categories had distinctly different soil properties. Frozen soils had much larger organic layers, and often mineral soils could not be detected. Dry sites had a thinner loamy surface layer compared to thawed sites. The data indicated that many wet soils do not thaw and become drier following fire, and that these sites tend to occur on concave, lower-slope positions and on northerly slope aspects. Convex, higher-slope positions and soils with a thin layer of loamy surface material likely remain dry and permafrost-free, regardless of the amount of time elapsed since fire. Post-fire vegetation changes were greatest on soils that thaw deeply, leading to more cover and forage for voles.

146. Swanson, D.K., 2010, Mapping of erosion features related to thaw of permafrost in Bering Land Bridge National Preserve, Cape Krusenstern National Monument, and Kobuk National Park: National Park Service, Fort Collins, Colorado, Natural Resource Data Series NPS/ARCN/NRDS—2010/122, 18 p.

This report presents results on the survey of active-layer detachment slides and thaw slumps in northwestern Alaska using high-resolution satellite imagery acquired from 2006 to 2008. There were a total of 58 detachment slides covering an area of 6 ha, and no reported thaw slumps in the study area.

147. Swanson, D.K., 2012, Mapping of erosion features related to thaw of permafrost in the Noatak National Preserve, Alaska: National Park Service, Fort Collins, Colorado. Natural Resource Data Series NPS/ARCN/NRDS—2012/248, 28 p.

This report presents results on the survey of active-layer detachment slides and thaw slumps in northwestern Alaska using high-resolution satellite imagery acquired from 2006 to 2008. There were a total of 848 detachment slides covering an area of 103 ha, most commonly on well vegetated, moderate slopes (average slope 16 percent) with a southwest aspect. A total of 276 thaw slumps were mapped covering an area of 90 ha. These features primarily occur on thick Pleistocene sediments (mainly glacial till and glacial lake deposits), primarily along rivers and lakes, though some occur in uplands away from water.

148. Swanson, D.K., 2012, Monitoring of retrogressive thaw slumps in the Arctic Network, 2011—Three-dimensional modeling of landform change: National Park Service, Fort Collins, Colorado, Natural Resource Report NPS/ARCN/NRDS—2012/247, 60 p.

This report presents results on a novel technique for monitoring retrogressive thaw slump dynamics in northwestern Alaska. Twenty-six thaw slumps were imaged in 2010 and again in 2011 using a hand-held 35-mm digital camera. The photographs were registered to features on the ground and used to create high-resolution, three-dimensional topographic models for change-detection analysis. The change in thaw-slump area ranged from negligible to about 1 ha between the 2 years. Headwall-retreat rates were less than 5 m in some cases but as much as 20 m in other cases. In the most active slump, the volume of subsidence was 30,000 m^3.

149. **Thienpont, J.R., R ü land, K.M., Pisaric, M.F., Kokelj, S.V., Kimpe, L.E., Blais, J.M., and Smol, J.P., 2013, Biological responses to permafrost thaw slumping in Canadian Arctic lakes: Freshwater Biology, p. 58, no. 2, p. 337–353.**

This paper uses a diatom-based palaeolimnological approach to examine the impact of retrogressive thaw slumps on freshwater ecosystems in the low Arctic of western Canada. Sediment cores were collected from the center of several lakes during 2007–2008 using a Glew-type gravity corer. Sediments were aged using lead-210 and cesium-137 radioisotopes and gamma dating. Sedimentary siliceous subfossils were analyzed to examine diatom abundance and composition. Affected and reference lakes were paired, and all of them showed biological changes over the last 200 years. Most reference sites showed an increase in the relative abundance of planktonic algal taxa beginning around 1900, consistent with increased temperature trends in the region. Thaw slump-affected lakes recorded increases in the abundance and diversity of periphytic diatoms around the time of slump initiation, consistent with increased water clarity and subsequent development of aquatic macrophyte communities. Additionally, all lakes showed a decrease in the relative abundance of benthic fragilarioid taxa correlated with local air temperature. Slump-affected lakes generally showed lower nutrient levels, except at a lake that had a slump as a result of an intense fire.

150. **Tondu, J.M., 2012, An interdisciplinary approach to monitoring the hydroecology of thermokarst lakes in Old Crow Flats, Yukon Territory, Canada: Waterloo, Canada, University of Waterloo, thesis.**

This thesis explains, in detail, methods for monitoring hydroecology of thermokarst lakes in Old Crow Flats, Yukon Territories, Canada. Water samples for analysis of hydrogen and oxygen isotope composition and chemistry (that is, ions and nutrients) were collected to track hydrological and limnological conditions. Artificial substrates were deployed in June and accrued algae were collected at the end of the ice-free season to assess community composition and abundance. Sediment coring was done in a culturally significant lake (Zelma Lake–OCF06) to reconstruct long-term baseline hydroecological conditions over the past three centuries. Radiometric dating techniques (cesium-137, lead-210) were used to develop a sediment core chronology. Baseline hydroecological conditions were reconstructed through analyses of loss-on-ignition, bulk organic carbon and nitrogen elemental and isotope compositions, and pigments. Meteorological data and a multi-year evaporation pan experiment were used to develop a robust isotope framework, which provides the basis for interpreting five years (2007–11) of lake water isotope measurements and deriving knowledge of hydrological conditions for the monitoring lakes. Three lakes showed a potential transition from snowmelt-sourced to rainfall-sourced isotope-based hydrologic regimes. Three lakes showed signs of being evaporation-dominated with positive water balances, and three lakes were evaporation-dominated with negative water balances. A multi-proxy paleolimnology analysis showed that lake conditions were stable until about 1900, then thermokarst expanded with a reduction in productivity until about 1943, and most recently Zelda Lake showed increased productivity and rapid drainage. The monitoring methods in this thesis already have been implemented by Parks Canada as a long-term hydroecological monitoring program for the Old Crow Flats area.

151. Toniolo, H., Kodial, P., Hinzman, L.D., and Yoshikawa, K., 2009, Spatio-temporal evolution of a thermokarst in interior Alaska: Cold Regions Science and Technology, v. 56, no. 1, p. 39–49.

This paper describes the rapid development of a thermokarst gully in interior Alaska over a two year period with a focus on the role of sediment transport and its associated geomorphological processes. The study combined the use of fieldwork and laboratory work. Fieldwork consisted of topographical surveys, discharge measurements, systematic water sampling, and abundant visual documentation of morphologic changes through digital photographs. Laboratory work mainly consisted of water-sample analyses to obtain suspended-solid concentration and suspended sediment grain-size distribution. The processes responsible for the rapid development of the features consisted of fluvio-thermal erosion and cryogenic piping. Headward erosion of the gully was 3.5 m/yr during the study period, and lateral slumping of the gully walls was 0.5 m/yr. Active sedimentation from the thermokarst has led to initial infilling of a pond in the drainage. Because groundwater flow in the study site was determined to be an important part of the accelerated thermokarst growth, future work should examine more closely the subsurface flow network.

152. Tsuyuzaki, S., Ishazaki, T., and Sato, T., 1999, Vegetation structure in gullies developed by the melting of ice wedges along Kolyma River, northern Siberia: Ecological Research, v. 14, no. 4, p. 385–391.

This paper examined the relationship between thermokarst gully characteristics and vegetation communities in northern Siberia, Russia. The authors surveyed 5–10 randomly selected plots within each gully. Height, width, and slope of each gully were measured with a transit compass and soil moisture and pH was tested using a portable soil tester. Soil compaction was tested at five points in each plot using a soil hardness tester. Percent cover of each plant species was visually estimated. In gullies surveyed, about 50 percent of the area was vegetated. Cluster analysis revealed four vegetation community types: (1) flixweed (*Descurainia sophia*)-dominated grassland, (2) chamomile (*Matricaria matricarioides*)-dominated forbland, (3) purple dropseed (*Agrostis purpurascens*)-dominated grassland with fire moss (*Ceratodon purpureus*) carpet, and (4) fireweed (*Chamaenerium angustifolium*)- and chamomile-dominated forbland. Gully height, width, and elevational differences influenced dominant vegetation types. The authors determined that these differences were mediated by the influence of gully height on soil pH and compaction and soil stability, which then influenced vegetation establishment. Dominant species were all long-distance dispersers, and the authors suggested revegetation of thermokarst features such as gullies favor species with long-distance dispersal mechanisms. Soil moisture was positively associated with soil pH and soil compaction. Steep slopes were composed of softer soils that is., less compact and stable). Flixweed was established in large gullies, while common horsetail (*Equisetum arvense*) and feltleaf willow (*Salix alaxensis*) was established in small gullies. Siberian dock (*Rumex sibericus*) were not established on compact soils, where fire moss was common. Fireweed and chamomile were not established on small gullies with soft soil and low soil pH.

153. Tsuyuzaki, S., Sawada, Y., Kushida, K., and Fukuda, M., 2008, A preliminary report on the vegetation zonation of palsas in the Arctic National Wildlife Refuge, northern Alaska, USA: Ecological Research, v. 23, no. 4, p. 787–793.

Vegetation, hydrologic parameters, and wildlife activity were monitored on 3 palsas. Vegetation zonation was observed to depend on water levels, with *Vaccinium vitis-idaea* on the top (drier part) of the palsas, *Carex aquatilis* near the bottom (wetter part) of the palsas, and *Sphagnum* spp. Significant autocorrelation was noted between the measured variables.

52

154. **Ugolini, F.C., 1975, Ice-rafted sediments as a cause of some thermokarst lakes in the Noatak River Delta, Alaska: New York, Science, v. 188, no. 4183 , p. 51-52.**
This paper describes the formation of thermokarst lakes as a result of ice-rafted sediment for a 7-km^2 area on the western part of the Noatak River Delta. This mechanism depends on the freezing of shallow lakes and channels to their bed and the incorporation of bottom sediments into the ice. During spring break-up or during fall storms, when sediment-rich ice bodies can migrate onto the landscape, this dirty ice is deposited. Following melt of the rafted ice deposits, the sediments that were entrained melt out and change the surface albedo and the thermal regime of the underlying soil promoting thaw and formation of thermokarst ponds. The entire sequence of the formation of thermokarst ponds through these processes has not been observed.

155. **Ulrich, M., Morgenstern, A., Günther, F., Reiss, D., Bauch, K.E., Hauber, E., and Schirrmeister, L., 2010, Thermokarst in Siberian ice-rich permafrost—Comparison to asymmetric scalloped depressions on Mars: Journal of Geophysical Research—Planets (1991–2012), v. 115, no. E10.**
This paper analyses a thermokarst depression in ice-rich Siberian yedoma deposits in the Lena river delta and compares results with remote sensing data from Martian surfaces. In Siberia, the authors did field studies on the morphometry of the thermokarst basin, described ground ice and lithologic compositions, and later did a GIS-based analysis of slope characteristics and a solar-insolation analysis to identify drivers of lateral thermokarst development in the basin. Fieldwork was done using a Zeiss ELTA C30 tachymeter, and multiple days were spent surveying the thermokarst basin in great detail to construct a digital elevation model. Vegetation, active layer, micro and mesorelief, and hydrological conditions were mapped further. Additionally, a pyranometer was used to quantify downwelling shortwave solar radiation. ArcGIS was used for the digital elevation model (DEM) creation and the solar insolation analysis. Modeled solar insolation also was compared to remote-sensed thermal data from Landst-7 Enhanced Thematic Mapper Plus (ETM+). The authors concluded from their analysis that the thermokarst basin and the lake located in the basin are expanding laterally northward.

156. **van Everdingen, Robert, ed., 1998 (revised May 2005), Multi-language glossary of permafrost and related ground-ice terms: Boulder, Colorado, National Snow and Ice Data Center, p. 1-46.**
This reference provides the most comprehensive index of permafrost- and ground-ice-related terminology. It can be accessed on the internet through the National Snow and Ice Data Center (NSIDC).

157. **Vincent, W.F., Callaghan, T.V., Dahl-Jensen, D., Johansson, M., Kovacs, K.M., Michel, C., and Sharp, M., 2011, Ecological implications of changes in the Arctic cryosphere: Ambio, v. 40, no. 1, p. 87–99.**
This paper is condensed from the ecology synthesis chapter of the Snow, Water, Ice, Permafrost in the Arctic (SWIPA) project of the Arctic Monitoring and Assessment Program. An overview is presented of how climate-dependent alterations in snow, water, ice, and permafrost are affecting, and will increasingly affect, the ecology of the Arctic, including potential effects from the linkages between ecosystems.

158. **Walker, D.A., Jia, G.J., Epstein, H.E., Raynolds, M.K., Chapin Iii, F.S., Copass, C., and Shiklomanov, N., 2003, Vegetation-soil-thaw-depth relationships along a low-arctic bioclimate gradient, Alaska—Synthesis of information from the ATLAS studies: Permafrost and Periglacial Processes, v. 14, no. 2, p. 103–123.**
This paper examines the interactions between summer warmth, vegetation, and thaw at 17 sites in three bioclimate subzones of the Arctic Slope and Seward Peninsula. Ground ice state is balanced by thawing related to warm air temperatures and freezing related to insulation by dense plant canopies. Warmer temperatures on a latitudinal gradient did not increase tussock tundra biomass as much as might be expected, indicating that growth is limited more by cold, wet soils than by air temperatures. The authors suggested that warming will not necessarily lead to thicker active layers because of the potential for additional insulation by growing plants. Soil pH also was found to influence plant production, with shallower thaw depths associated with acidic tundra.

159. **Walker, J., Arnborg, L., and Peippo, J., 1987, Riverbank erosion in the Colville Delta, Alaska: Geografiska Annaler—Series A—Physical Geography, p. 61–70.**
This paper summarizes the erosion rates of the Colville River Delta, Alaska. The delta is ice covered for more than 8 months a year, and is subjected to high discharge rates and periodic flooding events during ice break-up each year. Bank erosion is likely to occur along as much as 60 percent of the banks of the main river channels during the 3–4-week ice break-up period. Erosion is the result of hydromechanical and thermal impact of water as well as other factors including bank composition and height, snow and ice cover, stage and velocity of discharge, air and water temperature, and wind. Thermo-erosional niches form and large blocks break off into the river. The banks were measured during irregular time periods from 1961 to 1987. Echosounding traces were used to monitor the shifting of the channel and changes in channel form. Stakes were placed 25 or 50 ft from the bluff edge to measure erosion rates. During one particular year, erosion ranged from 0 to 10.9 m. Over a five year period, two stakes had been destroyed by erosion, three stakes were found over the bluff edge, and two stakes were missing. Most erosional banks were peat (75 percent), followed by laminated silts (15 percent); gubik silts, sands, and gravels (7 percent); and sand dunes (3 percent). Average erosion rates may have been as much as 4 m per year, but rarely exceeded 3 m per year, although there was high spatial and temporal variability. Block collapse can result in as much as 12 m of instantaneous retreat. The rate of break-up affects erosion rates; fast break-up may result in faster erosion rates.

160. **Wallace, R.E., 1948, Cave-in lakes in the Nabesna, Chisana, and Tanana River valleys, eastern Alaska: The Journal of Geology, p. 171–181.**
This paper attempts to identify the causes of thermokarst (that is, cave-in) lakes. The importance of vegetation as an insulator and of vegetation loss as the first step beginning the thermokarst process are recognized. Thermokarst lakes occur predominately in fine-grained sediments and not coarser materials. The authors created a conceptual sequence of thaw lake development with four ages: youthful, early mature, late mature, and old. Tilted and drowned trees were recognized as indicators of bank recession and as a mechanism for calculating lake expansion rates.

161. **West, J.J., and Plug, L.J., 2008, Time-dependent morphology of thaw lakes and taliks in deep and shallow ground ice: Journal of Geophysical Research, v. 113, no. F1, p. 1–14, F01009.**

This paper examines the shape and depth of thaw-lake basins in relation to lake age and stability of the talik. A numerical model was used for conductive heat transfer, phase change, and thaw subsidence of ice-rich sediment beneath a lake to estimate lake age. For lakes of all topography and ground-ice variations, first-generation lakes in deep ground ice are rounder and grow larger in area than later-generation lakes. Lake depth increases with about the square root of time in permafrost with a deep layer of excess ice. Large-diameter basins in icy permafrost are predicted to require about 5,000 years to reach depths of 20 m. A 1°C increase in lake-bottom temperature beyond the 3°C increase predicted in this climate model would increase the deepening rate of large lakes to 20 m in about 3,500 years. In contrast, lakes in permafrost with shallow epigenetic ground ice have depths that are independent of lake age. For these lakes, a steady-state depth is achieved within 100 years.

162. **White, D., Hinzman, L., Alessa, L., Cassano, J., Chambers, M., Falkner, K., Francis, J., Gutowski, W.J., Holland, M., Holmes, R.M., Huntington, H., Kane, D., Kliskey, A., Lee, C., McClelland, J., Peterson, B., Rupp, T.S., Staneo, F., Steele, M., Woodgate, R., Yang, D., Yoshikawa, K., and Zhang, T., 2007, The arctic freshwater system— Changes and impacts: Journal of Geophysical Research, v. 112, no. G4, G04S54.**

This paper reviews the effects of climate change on the Arctic freshwater system during the last century. It focuses on terrestrial, atmospheric, and oceanic systems. On land, precipitation and river discharge, lake abundance and size, glacier area and volume, soil moisture, and a variety of permafrost characteristics have changed. In the ocean, sea ice thickness and areal coverage have decreased and water mass circulation patterns have shifted, changing freshwater pathways and sea ice cover dynamics. Precipitation onto the ocean surface also has changed. Warming permafrost and subsequent thermokarst events are intimately tied to changes in terrestrial freshwater cycles. River discharge may change in ways not predictable from precipitation and evapotranspiration alone owing to changes in storage. Lakes may be expected to appear and grow in areas of continuous permafrost, while shrinking and disappearing in more degraded permafrost. A deeper active layer will have the capacity to attenuate peak flows of runoff owing to increased storage, and thermokarst geomorphology will create more heterogeneity in soil moisture, leading to ponding in some areas but drying in other areas. Complex feedbacks are expected, such as conditions more conducive to fire, which then lowers albedo and initially increases soil moisture.

163. **Wollschläger, U., Gerhards, H., Yu, Q., and Roth, K., 2010, Multi-channel ground-penetrating radar to explore spatial variations in thaw depth and moisture content in the active layer of a permafrost site: The Cryosphere, v. 4, no. 3, p. 269–283.**
This paper describes the use of multi-channel ground-penetrating radar (GPR) for measuring the active-layer thickness and moisture content at a continuous permafrost site on the Tibetan Plateau. Surveys were conducted on a grid that measured 85-by-60 m using three 200-megahertz antennas connected in a multi-channel configuration that allows for the simultaneous measure of travel time from many different antenna separations, which improves the ability to accurately measure target depths and soil moisture content. This configuration is an operational technology for efficiently studying surface permafrost dynamics at scales varying from a few meters to a few kilometers, and the multi-channel GPR technique efficiently covers the intermediate scales between traditional point measurements and space-based remote sensing.

164. **Yang, Z.P., Ou, Y.H., Xu, X.L., Zhao, L., Song, M.H., and Zhou, C.P., 2010, Effects of permafrost degradation on ecosystems: Acta Ecologica Sinica, v. 30, no. 1, p. 33–39.**
This paper reviews the effects of permafrost degradation on ecosystem structure and function, focusing primarily on research conducted on the Qinghai-Tibet Plateau, China. Permafrost degradation alters the water-heat process of soil, which leads to changes in vegetation species composition and community succession, and further ecosystem degradation. Additionally, degradation affects soil nutrient availability, and carbon storage in the Arctic and the Subarctic. Permafrost degradation may lead to improved soil drainage and active-layer depth, which are important controlling factors of vegetation growth and distribution. In Alaska, drier soils facilitated encroachment of shrubs and woody vegetation into tundra ecosystems. In the uplands of China, permafrost degradation led to increases in weedy vegetation and shifted from wet to drought-tolerant plant species, leading to a shift from a mesophyte-dominated alpine meadow ecosystem to an alpine desert steppe ecosystem and decreases in overall primary productivity. In ice-rich permafrost regions, degradation increased soil moisture and changed communities from terrestrial to aquatic. In Mentasta Pass and Tanana Flats, Alaska wet sedge meadows, bogs, and thermokarst lakes replaced forests. Thawing permafrost decreased the content of water-soluble nitrogen, potassium, and phosphorus in China, but other studies in Sweden showed permafrost degradation improved nitrogen mineralization and availability, and subsequent community productivity. Permafrost degradation also releases carbon and nitrogen dioxide (N_2O) currently stored in frozen soils and provides a positive feedback mechanism for further global warming. Increased plant growth may sequester some, but not all, of this excess carbon and nitrogen.

165. **Yoshikawa, K., and Hinzman, L.D., 2003, Shrinking thermokarst ponds and groundwater dynamics in discontinuous permafrost near Council, Alaska: Permafrost and Periglacial Processes, v. 14, no. 2, p. 151–160.**
This study used multiple field and laboratory techniques to better understand the dynamics of thermokarst lakes and to characterize groundwater infiltration and surface-water dynamics in an area of discontinuous permafrost near Council, Alaska (Seward Peninsula). The authors used synthetic aperture radar (SAR) data to classify terrain units and surface water properties, historical aerial photographs and satellite images (IKONOS) to assess pond shrinking and recent thermokarst progression, ground-penetrating radar (GPR) and DC resistivity to detect permafrost thickness and talik formations, and temperature boreholes and hydrological observation wells to ground truth their other methods. Thermokarst features had developed in many areas within the last 20 years. Thermokarst

lakes over ice-wedge terrain in the region have decreased in surface area since the early 20th century. Small thermokarst features developed into tundra ponds perched over permafrost, then grew larger and initiated large taliks that completely penetrated the permafrost, resulting in internal drainage throughout the year. Water budgets for several thermokarst lakes in the region were estimated and the complete drying of several lakes were predicted in the near future. In regions over thin, warm permafrost, surface ponds may shrink and newly developed small ponds may form. Surface soils may become drier as the permafrost degrades, with significant effects on latent and sensible heat fluxes (and subsequent vegetation characteristics and fire regimes). The authors suggested that, with further climate change, thermokarst lakes will continue to shrink in areas of discontinuous permafrost.

166. **Yoshikawa, K., Bolton, W.R., Romanovsky, V.E., Fukuda, M., and Hinzman, L.D., 2003, Impacts of wildfire on the permafrost in the boreal forests of interior Alaska: Journal of Geophysical Research, v. 108, no. D1, 8148.**
This paper examines the effect of wildfires on permafrost in the boreal forest of interior Alaska by studying 11 fire sites, including 2 controlled burns, with years of ignition ranging from 1924 to 2000. The authors focused particularly on quantifying the effects of fire on (1) direct heat conduction and convection to the ground, (2) removing moss as an insulating material, (3) heat budget, (4) soil moisture characteristics, and (5) active-layer thickness and talik formation. Immediately following fire, ground thermal conductivity may increase tenfold and the surface albedo can decrease by 50 percent depending on the extent of burning of the surficial organic soil. The authors determined that if the organic layer thickness was not reduced during the burn, then the active layer did not change after the burn in spite of the surface albedo decrease. However, for sites with a high burn severity and combustion of the organic layer, the active layer increased to a depth that did not refreeze each winter after a period of 3–5 years. At a site that burned in 1983, and talik thickness of 4 m was already present. An overview of the instrumentation involved in the study is given in table 1 of the study.

167. **Zhang, K., Kimball, J.S., Mu, Q., Jones, L.A., Goetz, S.J., and Running, S.W., 2009, Satellite based analysis of northern ET trends and associated changes in the regional water balance from 1983 to 2005: Journal of Hydrology, v. 379, no. 1, p. 92–110.**
This paper uses satellite remotely sensed inputs to drive an evapotranspiration (ET) algorithm for the Arctic and Alaska. The algorithm suggests a significant, increasing trend in ET with time. A weak increasing trend in precipitation and annual runoff suggest intensification of the pan-Arctic terrestrial water cycle during the 23-year period of record. The model displayed substantial spatial variability. Uncertainties exist because the model does not consider snow and ice sublimation during the frozen period, precipitation events, sparse precipitation observations, and the likely underestimation of open-water evaporation rates. Despite these potential sources of error, the model agreed well with tower-derived ET measurements. These results are consistent with other climate models, and with theoretical expectations given a warmer temperatures and more energy to drive the hydrologic cycle.

Russian-Language Literature

These references were taken from Shur and Osterkamp (2007). They have been included here for two reasons: (1) to demonstrate the long history of thermokarst-related research in the Russian literature, and (2) to provide a central and accessible location for these references in case some are translated to English in the future.

168. Are, F.E., 1969, On present-day drying of the thermokarst lakes in central Yakutia, *in* Geographical problems in Yakutia: Yakutsk, USSR (Russia), issue 5, p. 78–87. [In Russian.]

169. Are, F.E., 1985, Fundamentals of shore thermal-abrasion: Novosibirsk, USSR (Russia), Nauka. [In Russian.]

170. Are, F.E., Balobaev, V.T., and Bosikov, N.P., 1974, Peculiarities of shore erosion of thermokarst lakes in Central Yakutia, in Lakes of Cryolitozone of Siberia: Novosibirsk, USSR (Russia), Nauka, p. 39–52. [In Russian.]

171. Bakulin, F.G., 1958, Ice content and thaw settlement of perennially frozen Quaternary deposit of the Vorkuta region: Moscow, USSR Academy of Sciences Press. [In Russian.]

172. Bosikov, N.P., 1996, Climate change and thermokarst evolution, in Climate impact on permafrost landscapes of central Yakutia: Yakutsk, Russia, Permafrost Institute, p. 106–121. [In Russian.]

173. Boytsov, M.N., 1965, Evolution of the thermokarst lakes basins, in Anthropogenic period in Arctic and Subarctic: Moscow, Nedra, p. 327–339. [In Russian.]

174. Durdenevskaya, M.V., 1932, Permafrost and ground ice in lake shores in the Irkut river valley, Commission on Permafrost Study, vol. 1: Leningrad (St. Petersburg), USSR Academy of Sciences, p. 55–67. [In Russian.]

175. Efimov, A.I., 1946, Drying of the thermokarst lakes of central Yakutia: Merzlotovedenie, vol. 1, no. 2, p. 95–105. [In Russian.]

176. Ermolaev, M.M., 1932, Geology and geomorphology of the Bol'shoy Liakhovsky Island, in Polar geophysical station at the Bol'shoy Liakhvsky Island: Leningrad (St. Petersburg), USSR Academy of Sciences, p. 147–228. [In Russian.]

177. Fel'dman, G.M., 1984, Thermokarst and permafrost: Novosibirsk, USSR (Russia), Nauka. [In Russian.]

178. Kachurin, S.P., 1961, Thermokarst in the USSR: Moscow, USSR Academy of Sciences Press. [In Russian.]

179. Katasonov, E.M., 1978, Thermokarst as historic-geological process: *in* General Permafrost—Articles submitted to Third International Conference on Permafrost: Novosibirsk, USSR (Russia), Nauka, p. 124–130. [In Russian.]

180. Katasonov, E.M., 1979, About thermokarst and thermokarst forms of relief, *in* Structures and age of alas deposit of central Yakutia: Novosibirsk, USSR (Russia), Nauka, p. 4–7. [In Russian.]

181. Mukhin, N.I., 1960, Importance of the polygonal forms of relief for thermokarst development in Low Indigirka River area, *in* A collection of articles on fundamentals of geocryology: Moscow, USSR Academy of Sciences Press, p. 41–55. [In Russian.]

182. Pchelintsev, A.M., 1946, Morphologic description of the thermokarst in Yakutia, *in* A collection of articles of the Permafrost Institute: v. 1, no. 2, p. 95–105. [In Russian.]

183. Shur, Y.L., 1977, Thermokarst (on thermo-physical fundamentals of the thermokarst development): Moscow, Nedra, 80 p. [In Russian.]

184. Shur, Y.L., 1981, Thermokarst prediction, *in* Recommendations on prediction of permafrost related geological processes in developing areas of Far North: Moscow, All-Russian Research Institute for Hydrogeology and Engineering Geology (VSEGINGEO), p. 16–35. [In Russian.]

185. Shur, Y.L., 1983, Prediction of thermokarst *in* Grechishchev, S.E., ed., Geocryological prediction for West Siberia Natural Gas Province: Novosibirsk, USSR (Russia), Nauka, p. 210–226. [In Russian.]

186. Shur, Y.L., 1988, The upper horizon of permafrost and thermokarst: Novosibirsk, Russia, Nauka, 210 p. [In Russian.]

187. Shur, Y.L., Petrukhin, N.P., and Slavin-Borovskiy, V.B., 1978, Shore erosion in the permafrost region, *in* Permafrost related processes: Moscow, Nauka, p. 57–74. [In Russian.]

188. Soloviev, P.A., 1962, Alas relief of central Yakutia and its origin, *in* Grave, N.A., ed., Permafrost and related features in central Yakutia: Moscow, USSR Academy of Sciences Press, p. 38–54. [In Russian.]

189. Soloviev, P.A., 1973, Alas thermokarst relief of central Yakutia, Guidebook: Second International Conference on Permafrost, Yakutsk, USSR (Russia), 48 p. [In Russian.]

190. Stremyakov A. Ya., 1963, On genesis of oriented lakes—Permafrost in different regions of the USSR: USSR Academy of Sciences, p. 75–107. [In Russian.]

191. Sukhodrovskiy, V.L., 1979, Exogenic relief formation in the permafrost region: Moscow, Nauka, 279 p. [In Russian.]

192. Uvarkin, Y.T., 1969, Recommendations on thermokarst investigations during geotechnical survey in the permafrost region: Moscow, PNIIIS.

193. Uvarkin, Y.T., and Shamanova, I.I., 1973, Main regularities of the thermokarst development in west Siberia, Second International Conference on Permafrost, Yakutsk, USSR (Russia), issue 2, p. 142–145. [In Russian.]

194. Velmina, N.A., 1957, Origin of closed (alas) depressions in central Yakutia , *in* Permafrost conditions of west Siberia, Yakutia, and Chukotka: Moscow, Nauka, p. 37–71. [In Russian.]

195. Vturin, B.I., 1975, Underground ice in the USSR: Moscow, Nauka. [In Russian.]

Acknowledgments

Funding for this work was largely provided by grant 2012-15 from the Arctic Landscape Conservation Cooperative provided to the U.S. Geological Survey–Alaska Science Center. Additional support was provided by the U.S. Geological Survey–Alaska Science Center, the U.S. Geological Survey–Land Change Science program, and the University of Alaska–Fairbanks–Permafrost Laboratory. A special thanks to M. Torre Jorgenson, Kenneth M. Hinkel, and Yuri Shur for reviewing version 1.0 and to John Osias and Linda Rogers for editing the bibliography.

www.ingramcontent.com/pod-product-compliance
Lightning Source LLC
Chambersburg PA
CBHW080441290526
45791CB00008BA/2571